REIMAGINING SCHOOL CLIMATE

Creating the Conditions for Safety, Support, Value, and Fulfillment

Mario I. Acosta   Tina H. Boogren

Solution Tree | Press
a division of Solution Tree

AI outputs featured in the text and figure I.2 generated with the assistance of ChatGPT.

555 North Morton Street
Bloomington, IN 47404
800.733.6786 (toll free) / 812.336.7700
FAX: 812.336.7790

email: info@SolutionTree.com
SolutionTree.com

Visit **go.SolutionTree.com/schoolimprovement** to download the free reproducibles in this book.

Printed in the United States of America

FSC
www.fsc.org
MIX
Paper | Supporting responsible forestry
FSC® C008955

Library of Congress Control Number: 2026009673
ISBN: 979-8-89374-117-9

Solution Tree
Cameron L. Rains, CEO
Edmund M. Ackerman, President

Solution Tree Press
Publisher: Kendra Slayton
Associate Publisher: Todd Brakke
Acquisitions Director: Hilary Goff
Editorial Director: Laurel Hecker
Art Director: Rian Anderson
Managing Editor: Sarah Ludwig
Copy Chief: Jessi Finn
Senior Production Editor: Christine Hood
Copy Editor: Charlotte Jones
Proofreader: Elijah Oates
Text and Cover Designer: Rian Anderson
Content Development Specialist: Amy Rubenstein
Associate Editor: Elijah Oates
Editorial Assistant: Madison Chartier

Acknowledgments

I want to begin by thanking my friend and coauthor, Tina Boogren, for joining me in this project. Tina is not only a world-class educator but also one of the most thoughtful and skilled authors and trainers in our field. I am deeply grateful for her partnership, mentorship, and the countless ways she strengthened my writing throughout this process. It was an absolute thrill to collaborate with her.

I am also grateful to my wife, Courtney Acosta, who graciously listened to countless ideas for this book and offered encouragement and thoughtful feedback along the way. Her support and insight mean more than she knows.

—Mario I. Acosta

I'm deeply grateful to my coauthor, Mario Acosta. Mario brings a deep and steady understanding of school culture that comes from years of leading in schools and working alongside educators and students. He sees both the big picture and the small moments that shape how people experience school each day. This book is stronger because of his perspective.

I am also grateful to the educators and school leaders who continue to invite us into their work. They are the reason this book exists. Every time they share what is going well, what feels hard, or what they're still trying to figure out, they help us understand school climate in a deeper way. They also remind us that supporting school culture and supporting educator wellness are inseparable.

Schools are human places. They are shaped by relationships, effort, and the daily choice to care for one another. When adults feel supported and valued, they are better able to support students. I see that happening in schools across the United States, and it gives me hope.

—Tina H. Boogren

Finally, we would like to thank Amy Rubenstein, Christine Hood, Laurel Hecker, and the entire Solution Tree Press team for their guidance and commitment to bringing this book to life.

—Mario I. Acosta and Tina H. Boogren

Solution Tree Press would like to thank the following reviewers:

Zachary Ashauer
Social Sciences Teacher
Hortonville Area School District
Hortonville, Wisconsin

Drew Bowman
Mental Health Education Specialist
Headwater Learning Foundation
Calgary, Alberta, Canada

Molly Capps
Director of Student Support Services
Moore County Schools
Carthage, North Carolina

Anthony S. Golding
Principal
Pierce Street Elementary School
Tupelo, Mississippi

Jed Kees
Director of School Improvement Services
Cooperative Educational Service Agency No. 4
West Salem, Wisconsin

Pamela Liebenberg
Former Director of Curriculum and Instruction
Tuscaloosa County School System
Tuscaloosa, Alabama

Kelly Mack Outridge
Principal
Blenman Elementary School
Tucson, Arizona

Kirby Maness
Principal
Ayden-Grifton High School
Ayden, North Carolina

Chris Siegle
Assistant Principal
Robert Thirsk High School
Calgary, Alberta, Canada

Jill Thompson
International Baccalaureate Primary Years Program Coordinator
Charter Oak International Academy
West Hartford, Connecticut

Visit **go.SolutionTree.com/schoolimprovement** to download the free reproducibles in this book.

Table of Contents

Reproducibles are in italics.

About the Authors

Mario I. Acosta, EdD, is an award-winning educator, accomplished author, and highly regarded speaker and consultant. He spent twenty years of his educational career as a teacher, instructional coach, assistant principal, academic director, and principal leading schools with diverse profiles in the state of Texas. He was named the 2022 Texas principal of the year while principal of Westwood High School, a *U.S. News & World Report* Top 50 campus and member of the High Reliability Schools network.

Dr. Acosta has had success in leading schools of all sizes with students and teachers from a variety of backgrounds, communities, and socioeconomic statuses. He has led school turnarounds in high-poverty schools throughout Texas at both the middle and high school levels, which yielded immediate and significant growth in student achievement. Further, under his leadership, Westwood High School was recognized as a top 1 percent campus in the United States for academic achievement and college and career readiness.

Dr. Acosta is the author of *The Schools Our Students Deserve: A Comprehensive Framework for Shaping Exceptional School Culture*, the coauthor of several books, including *Five Big Ideas for Leading a High Reliability School* with Robert J. Marzano and Philip B. Warrick, and a contributor to the edited volumes *Culture Champions: Teachers Supporting a Healthy Classroom Culture*, *Culture Keepers: Leaders Creating a Healthy School Culture*, and *Professional Learning Communities at Work and High-Reliability Schools: Cultures of Continuous Learning.*

In 2022, Dr. Acosta joined the Marzano Resources and Solution Tree teams and works as an author and national presenter. He specializes in campus-level implementation of effective culture, High Reliability Schools (HRS), professional learning communities (PLCs), instructional improvement, response to intervention (RTI), effective teaching strategies for English learners, and standards-referenced reporting. As an HRS certifier, Dr. Acosta works with K–12 schools and districts across the United States as they progress through the levels of certification. He also serves as an adjunct professor in the educational leadership master's degree program at the University of Texas at Austin.

Dr. Acosta earned a bachelor's degree in mathematics from the University of Texas at Austin and a master's degree in educational leadership from Lamar University in Beaumont, Texas. He holds a doctorate in educational administration from the University of Texas at Austin and a superintendent certification in the state of Texas.

To learn more about Mario I. Acosta's work, follow him @theedleadershippair on YouTube and TikTok, and @edleadership_pair on Instagram. Dr. Acosta also co-hosts *The EdLeadership Pair* podcast (www.theedleadershippair.com), dedicated to helping today's school leaders navigate the complex realities of educational leadership.

Tina H. Boogren, PhD, is a fierce advocate for educators and an award-winning educator, best-selling author, and highly sought-after speaker. Dr. Boogren has proudly served as a classroom teacher, mentor, instructional coach, and building-level leader and presented to audiences all over the world.

Dr. Boogren is deeply committed to supporting educators so they can support their students. She conducts highly requested and inspiring keynotes, workshops, and virtual webinars that focus on quality instruction, coaching, mentoring, and educator wellness, and she hosts a weekly podcast, *Everyday Wellness With Dr. Tina H. Boogren*. Additionally, she is codirector of Solution Tree's Wellness Solutions for Educators with Timothy D. Kanold.

Dr. Boogren was a 2007 finalist for Colorado Teacher of the Year and was a recipient of her school district's Outstanding Teacher Award eight years in a row, from 2002 to 2009. She has been recognized as number five of the Top 30 Global Gurus in Education, is a Marquis Who's Who in America and Who's Who of Professional

Women recipient. She was also recognized in *The Wall Street Journal* among the Who's Who of Distinguished Leaders.

She is the author of numerous books, including *In the First Few Years: Reflections of a Beginning Teacher*; *Supporting Beginning Teachers*; *The Beginning Teacher's Field Guide: Embarking on Your First Years*; *180 Days of Self-Care for Busy Educators*; *Take Time for You: Self-Care Action Plans for Educators*, which was an Independent Publisher Book Awards gold winner in the Education category; and *Coaching for Educator Wellness: A Guide to Supporting New and Experienced Teachers*. She is coauthor of *Educator Wellness: A Guide for Sustaining Physical, Mental, Emotional, and Social Well-Being* with Timothy D. Kanold; *The Educator Wellness Plan Book and Journal* with Timothy D. Kanold and Jasmine K. Kullar; and *Motivating and Inspiring Students: Strategies to Awaken the Learner* with Robert J. Marzano, Darrell Scott, and Ming Lee Newcomb. She is a contributor to *Women Who Lead: Insights, Inspiration, and Guidance to Grow as an Educator*, edited by Janel Keating and Jasmine K. Kullar.

Dr. Boogren holds a bachelor's degree from the University of Iowa, a master's degree with an administrative endorsement from the University of Colorado Denver, and a doctorate in educational administration and policy studies from the University of Denver. Additionally, she is a Level 1 Certified nutrition coach and a specialist in change psychology through Precision Nutrition. She holds a women's coaching specialist certification through Girls Gone Strong and is currently pursuing personal training certification through the National Council on Strength and Fitness.

To learn more about Tina H. Boogren's work, follow her @THBoogren on X and Instagram, join her Facebook group (www.facebook.com/selfcarefor educators), and listen to her podcast, *Everyday Wellness With Dr. Tina H. Boogren* (www.tinaboogren.com).

To book Mario I. Acosta or Tina H. Boogren for professional development, contact pd@SolutionTree.com.

Introduction

There's a rhythm to every school.

It pulses in the energy of the hallways, classroom conversations, and the way we greet one another at the front doors. Some schools hum with a sense of belonging, hope, and calm. Others feel different—quiet in the wrong ways or loud in ways that make your chest tighten. Whether spoken or unspoken, this rhythm—the way a school *feels*—is what we call *school climate*. And make no mistake: Climate matters.

As educators, we know this instinctively. We feel it in our bones. But in this book, we'll go deeper than just "knowing." We'll explore what the research tells us: What we cultivate in our classrooms, hallways, staff lounges, and leadership practices determines the climate that unfolds. And in turn, that climate determines what's possible for our students and for ourselves and ultimately, the culture.

This is not just theoretical knowledge. It's not about mere decorations on walls or feel-good slogans on our posters. A robust school climate is the foundation that underpins everything we value: learning, growth, equity, well-being, and long-term success. When we effectively manage the school climate, the results are not just significant but tangible in our daily interactions and the overall school culture.

A robust school climate is the foundation that underpins everything we value: learning, growth, equity, well-being, and long-term success.

How We Feel in School and Why It Matters

School climate is, at its heart, about how we *feel*.

It's the emotional weather that envelops us every day. It's the invisible force that either lifts our spirits or weighs us down. A positive climate doesn't just make school a more pleasant place; it fundamentally shapes our ability to teach, learn, connect, and grow. Feelings of safety, support, and value aren't just nice-to-haves but are, in fact, the bedrock of deep engagement and sustainable success.

Humans are emotional beings first and cognitive beings second. When individuals feel safe and valued, their brains are primed for learning, creativity, and connection. Conversely, feeling unsafe, invisible, or exhausted can diminish one's capacity to engage effectively. Research indicates that a sense of safety reduces the brain's threat response, facilitating improved cognitive functioning and fostering creativity (Leadership HQ, 2025). Moreover, the concept of "Maslow before Bloom" underscores that meeting basic emotional needs is a prerequisite for effective learning because toxic stress can impair the brain's ability to process and retain information (Imad, 2022).

To understand climate is to understand the emotional life of a school. Honoring that emotional life is the first step toward creating a thriving school culture.

How Climate Impacts Schools

School climate is the collective heartbeat of a school, the emotional and relational atmosphere that impacts the quality of interactions among students, teachers, and staff (Asif & Shahbaz, 2025). It includes everything from safety and belonging to the learning environment and leadership practices. It is both tangible and intangible. You can work to measure it in student surveys, teacher retention, and attendance rates, and you can feel it in the air.

At its best, school climate reflects a space where people are known, valued, and challenged to grow. It's a non-negotiable, a prerequisite for real achievement (Darling-Hammond & Cook-Harvey, 2018).

Imagine, if you will, a cold and dark Monday morning; you've hit the snooze button on your phone twice already, and you are on the verge of being late for school. Today is a state testing day, and you somehow drew the short straw: You've been assigned to be on bathroom duty. The very last thing on earth you want to do now is leave the comfort of your warm bed to go to work in the student bathroom. You arrive at school with no time to catch your breath and spend the entire day feeling sluggish and disengaged, wondering if you should look for a new job.

Now, imagine that it is lunchtime on Friday of that very same week. Testing is done, and the lesson you have been teaching today is going great! Your students are engaged, happy, and truly learning. You enthusiastically engage in the final two hours of your workday, pouring every ounce of educational passion into the students you serve. After work, you meet your colleagues for some well-deserved rest and recovery time at your favorite after-work hangout spot. You feel fantastic and couldn't imagine doing any job other than this one.

If you've been teaching for any length of time, chances are you have experienced what each of these scenarios feels like. Most likely, it's all of us. These scenarios illustrate climate. School climate is how both students and adults feel sitting in class, walking through the halls, attending meetings, or engaging in their work (The Aspen Institute, 2021). Think of these experiences as the "emotional weather" of the organization, shifting and changing constantly with all the varied interactions and daily experiences that occur within the workday and change the moment-to-moment feelings of those within it. In the context of schools, climate manifests itself in the everyday interactions between staff and students (adult to student), between school leaders and the staff (adult to adult), among the student body (student to student), and among staff themselves (adult to adult). Every word, glance, policy, and pause either strengthens or strains the climate we create.

Climate is both a mirror of current organizational health and a lever for transformation, reacting to not only the perceptions of policies, daily practices, and common procedures, but also to the behaviors that are rewarded and expected within a group (Schneider, Ehrhart, & Macey, 2011). To gain a window through which to observe the organization's climate, we must examine the way every policy, procedure, and interaction influences how the people within the organization feel about their educational experience, work environment, and even the mood of the organization's culture, which Mario I. Acosta (2026) describes as the collective beliefs and resultant behavioral norms.

School climate is complex and dynamic. Because it is a construct based on people's feelings, it is not static; it is ever-shifting, constantly impacted by external pressures and internal interactions, and therefore, must be managed with an understanding of its constant fluidity. School climate shifts with changes in administrative support, working conditions, policy implications, interpersonal interactions, student behaviors, and external influences (Wang, Degol, & Henry, 2019).

As any educator can attest, school climate is so fluid that the time of year and even the day of the week can have an impact on it. The various phases of a school year significantly influence how teachers feel as they experience predictable emotional highs and lows aligned with the academic calendar. Picture a fourth-grade teacher who, in September, arrives early each morning and is brimming with fresh ideas and excitement for a new group of students. By February, that same teacher feels emotionally drained, less creative in lesson planning, and overwhelmed by behavior challenges and testing demands. This teacher is experiencing the predictable midyear dip emphasized by Timothy D. Kanold and Tina H. Boogren (2022), who describe how early enthusiasm in the fall can give way to fatigue and stress midyear, negatively impacting educators' well-being and effectiveness.

Climate fluidity also manifests daily as employees in all fields, not just educators, typically feel less satisfied and perceive more negative interactions at the start of the week with improvements as the week progresses. Employees report lower job satisfaction and higher perceptions of incivility on Mondays compared to Fridays, supporting the notion of the "Monday Blues" (Pindek, Zhou, Kessler, Krajcevska, & Spector, 2021). Consider a staff lounge on a Monday morning: A high school teacher notices her colleagues are quieter than usual, offering fewer greetings and engaging in less small talk with one another as they grab their coffee and go straight to their classrooms. By Friday, she sees those colleagues chatting, laughing, and sharing stories with one another before heading back to their classrooms, thus illustrating how emotional tone and interpersonal energy (and therefore, climate) can shift over the course of a week.

The fluidity of school climate is also evident in its ability, or inability, to adapt to external pressures placed on the organization. For instance, Pallavi Kumari and Anjan Niyogi (2025) note that organizational climates shifted significantly in the wake of the COVID-19 shutdowns with increased emphasis on employee well-being and psychological safety (which is a good thing). In schools, this fluidity can be observed in how quickly environments can deteriorate or improve based on leadership decisions, policy changes, election results, and parent or community engagement. For example, a school that encountered increased teacher burnout after the COVID-19 pandemic shutdown returned to in-person classes and quickly instituted weekly wellness check-ins and shortened staff meetings. They also created dedicated spaces for staff to decompress during the day, thus purposely creating a shift in school climate that prioritized psychological safety and well-being. Similarly, after returning to in-person learning, another school launched a mentoring initiative in which veteran teachers were paired with newer staff to rebuild connection and trust. Regular team-building sessions and shared planning time created a climate of mutual support, helping staff reestablish strong professional relationships and enhancing collaboration across grade levels.

Tending to school climate is not a one-time event or a single initiative; it is a daily, ongoing commitment. From the tone of each staff meeting to how student and adult successes are celebrated, every interaction shapes the emotional environment of the school. By actively working to be aware of and shape the climate, educators can transform schools into places where everyone, including both adults and students, can thrive.

The Relationship Between Culture and Climate

School culture and school climate are interconnected yet distinct concepts that influence the functioning of schools. While both shape the experiences of students, teachers, and administrators, they differ in their nature, formation, and impact. Just like people often confuse latitude and longitude, sympathy and empathy, or equality and equity, climate and culture are frequently and incorrectly used interchangeably. It is vital to understand how these differ from one another. One helpful way to understand the difference is through the analogy of the weather and the seasons (Gruenert & Whitaker, 2023).

School climate is about how adults and students experience daily school life (Acosta, 2026). Like the weather, it is what we feel on any given day and can change very quickly based on things like unexpected schedule changes, decisions made by the team leader, or student behaviors at lunchtime. Like the weather, school and classroom climate can be warm, stormy, calm, or stifling, depending on what's going on at any given moment. It shifts quickly and reflects the immediate perceptions and feelings of everyone in the building.

School culture, on the other hand, is like the *seasons* (winter, spring, summer, and fall). It represents the long-term patterns and norms that define the school's identity. Acosta (2026) explains:

> The school's culture encompasses beliefs and behaviors that are cultivated over time, honored by tradition, and validated by the shared experiences of educators, students, and the community alike. It reflects the school's character, a blueprint of its values, a defender of its present self, and a guide to its future. It is this persona that creates the boundaries of safety and normalcy for its members. (p. 12)

Just as you wouldn't expect winter to turn into summer overnight (we need spring first), school culture doesn't change with a single initiative or policy.

When educators and leaders are aware of and attend to the climate of their classroom or building with intention, day by day, they shape the conditions that gradually influence the school's culture. A couple of sunny days in a row doesn't necessarily change the season you are in, but sustained warmth over time signals a transition into a new season. If we neglect school climate, it allows toxic patterns to take root and will eventually alter culture in negative ways. Understanding this dynamic empowers schools to approach improvement as both immediate and sustained work and to use daily climate cues as indicators and levers for meaningful, lasting cultural change.

Consider figure I.1, which illustrates the relationship between climate and culture.

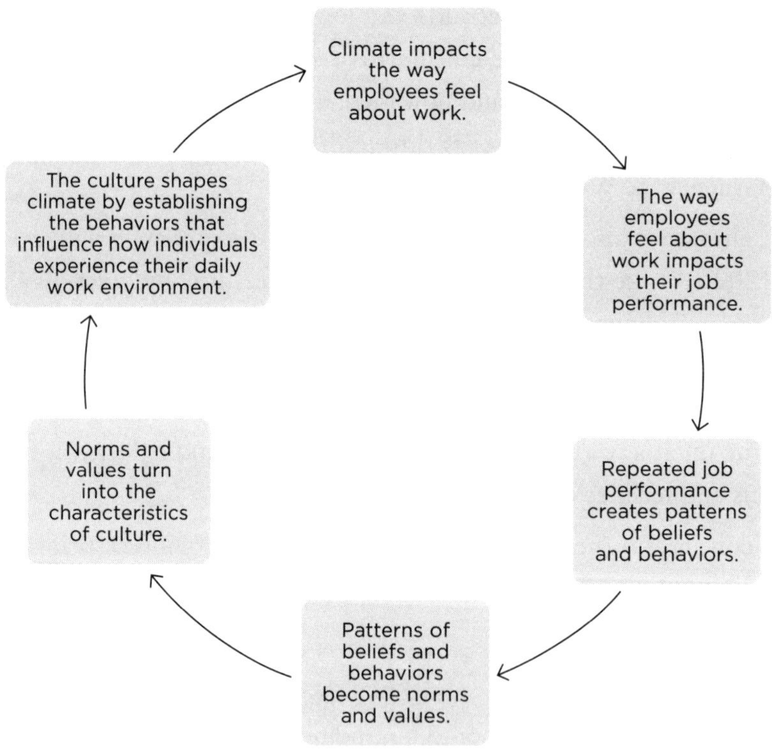

Source: Acosta, 2026, p. 122.

Figure I.1: The reciprocal relationship between climate and culture.

Climate is a driver of culture; the short term becomes the long term. Climate is what people feel today; culture is what they come to expect tomorrow based on what happened in the past. When school leaders and educators tend to the daily weather, when they ensure that adults and students experience positive feelings, such as safety, support, value, and fulfillment, they lay the foundation for a season—a culture—that reflects those same values and feelings. And just as meteorologists use weather patterns to predict the coming season, school leaders can look to climate patterns to forecast and intentionally shape their school's future.

The Relationship Between Self-Care or Educator Wellness and Climate

Self-care and educator wellness are deeply personal, internal experiences centered on how we feel, how we manage our own energy, and how we sustain our passion for the work. To show up as our best selves every day, we must tend to our physical, mental, and emotional health and well-being. When educators engage in intentional self-care practices, such as focusing on mindfulness to regulate their emotions, setting boundaries so they don't get stretched too thin, and prioritizing their physical wellness, they are better equipped to navigate classroom challenges and maintain positive relationships with students (Kanold & Boogren, 2022). Research since 2015 shows that teachers who prioritize emotional self-care report lower levels of burnout, which in turn leads to higher job satisfaction and stronger retention (321 Insight, n.d.). Simply put, when we take care of ourselves, we increase our capacity to stay in the profession, reduce turnover, and provide the consistency our students need.

Beyond the individual level, school climate refers to the collective atmosphere of a school—how it feels to be there, shaped by how individuals attend to the feelings and experiences of others, both adults and students. A positive school climate is one where teachers feel valued, respected, and connected within a collaborative community (Reisinger, 2024). This includes fostering strong relationships with colleagues, engaging in open communication, and participating in shared decision making, all of which contribute to a nurturing environment. Studies have shown that students who perceive their school climate as positive are less likely to experience emotional distress and more likely to report a sense of belonging and acceptance, which are critical factors to mental health and well-being (Strobel Education, 2023).

Individual self-care isn't a luxury for educators; instead, it's the quiet engine that powers a healthy school climate. When teachers and staff consistently tend to their own physical, emotional, and mental well-being, they create the internal stability needed to show up with presence, patience, and compassion. This personal foundation ripples outward: Regulated adults de-escalate conflict more effectively, build stronger relationships, and model resilience for both students and colleagues. In other words, caring for ourselves isn't separate from caring for our schools. By caring for ourselves, we establish a strong foundation for a positive school climate.

The Essential Feelings of a Positive School Climate

When educators describe the climate of their schools, they often talk about policies, programs, or systems. Yet beneath those structures lies something more human: how people feel when they walk through the doors each day. Students and educators constantly interpret their environment through emotional cues. As we examined the research on effective school climate, a consistent pattern emerged: The health of a school climate can ultimately be understood through a small set of core feelings that shape how people experience their work and learning.

Research confirms what many of us know instinctively: People thrive when they feel safe, supported, valued, and fulfilled. Across sectors, from healthcare to K–12 schools to corporate workplaces, well-designed environments that cultivate these emotional conditions consistently produce stronger engagement, resilience, satisfaction, and performance. This is not philosophical intuition; it is empirical reality. In fact, an American Psychological Association (2023) report found that 92 percent of U.S. workers say it is important to work for an organization that values their emotional and psychological well-being, yet only 57 percent feel their current employer actually does so. This gap matters: Employees who reported feeling safe, valued, and supported were more than twice as likely to say they perform at their best and three times more likely to report excellent mental health.

Researchers Karen T. Hallam, Natasha Popovic, and Leila Karimi (2023) find that when employees work within psychologically safe environments, they innovate more effectively and operate with greater focus and cohesion. Closely tied to safety is the experience of support, which emerges when people know that help, encouragement, and resources will be available when needed. Supportive workplaces, those that value personal strengths and growth, predict higher long-term well-being and capability (Weziak-Bialowolska et al., 2023). In education specifically, teachers report higher satisfaction, lower burnout, and stronger emotional stability when their working conditions provide relational support, clear structures, and opportunities for connection (Steiner, Woo, Suryavanshi, & Redding, 2023). For newer educators, an effective climate is even more acute. Elizabeth E. Heilman (2025) notes that early-career teachers' emotional well-being depends heavily on meeting their needs for belonging, safety, and affirmation. Without these experiences of safety and support, people disconnect.

Humans also need to feel valued. Feeling valued has a direct link to stronger well-being, higher motivation, deeper workplace commitment, and retention (Hall et al., 2024). Workers overwhelmingly identify "being valued by my employer" as one of the most important predictors of workplace well-being and production (American Psychological Association, 2023). When individuals sense that their contributions matter, they invest more fully in their work and in the collective mission. Feeling valued is an empirically validated driver of organizational success.

Ultimately, for humans to thrive, they must feel fulfilled—the sense that one's efforts have meaning and align with their individual values or goals. Work that feels purposeful and psychologically nourishing is linked to higher engagement, stronger performance, greater resilience, and increased retention (Martela et al., 2021). Fulfillment is what transforms effort from draining to energizing.

The emotional climate of an organization is foundational to the success of its people. When schools and school leaders intentionally cultivate environments where individuals feel safe, supported, valued, and fulfilled, they not only improve climate but also unlock human potential. In fact, studies show that factors like supportive leadership, recognition, and psychological safety are stronger drivers of engagement than perks or even pay alone (American Psychological Association, 2023; Gallup, 2023).

When schools and school leaders intentionally cultivate environments where individuals feel safe, supported, valued, and fulfilled, they not only improve climate but also unlock human potential.

Supportive leadership sets the tone. When leaders listen with empathy, follow through on promises, and foster trust, individuals are more likely to be engaged and satisfied (Mala, Abdullah, & Nento, 2022). This trust creates a strong foundation where open communication can flourish. Feeling truly heard helps individuals, both adults and students, feel safe enough to contribute ideas, ask for support, and grow (Rasheed et al., 2024). In schools, the consistency of communication and feedback translates to stronger student engagement and higher teacher morale (Xu, Haratyan, & Tian, 2026).

But trust and feedback aren't enough on their own. Individuals need to be recognized for their efforts and given room to grow. When we are acknowledged and offered opportunities to develop, whether through training, mentorship, professional learning opportunities, or simply a "thank you," engagement and sense of purpose deepen (Kraft, Blazar, & Hogan, 2018). If we add the absolute necessity of physical and emotional safety, both being protected from harm and being welcomed to show up as our full selves, we will start to see the full picture of what makes people *feel* good (McKinsey & Company, 2023).

At the core of it all are relationships: both adult-to-adult and adult-to-student relationships. As social beings, we're wired for connection. Camaraderie, collaboration, and belonging are essential for resilience, overall well-being, and joy (Gallup, 2023). And when we are trusted to do our work with autonomy, have a voice in decisions, and are supported in maintaining balance between work and life, our sense of ownership and pride skyrocket (Fernet, Morin, Mueller, Gillet, & Austin, 2023). For educators, this might mean flexibility in curriculum design, shared leadership structures, and the time and space to recharge.

And finally, there is the need for purpose. Knowing the *why* behind our work remains one of the most powerful motivators and helps us feel fulfilled. Fulfillment underpins deeper psychological engagement and transforms effort into meaningful contributions (Kenny, Medvide, & Gordon, 2024). When we believe our work matters, we show up differently.

In every corner of this research, one truth shines through: People, whether administrators, teachers, or students, flourish in environments that see them, support them, and help them grow. Qualitatively, the American Psychological Association (2023) report notes that people who feel psychologically safe, heard, and appreciated are more engaged, more resilient, and more committed to their organization. These findings reinforce a consistent pattern across research: When environments, especially classrooms, hallways, and school buildings, attend to core emotional needs of safety, support, value, and fulfillment, people thrive, and when they do not, performance and well-being erode.

Based on these findings, we believe that a positive school and classroom climate can be distilled down to four essential feelings: (1) feeling safe, (2) feeling supported, (3) feeling valued, and (4) feeling fulfilled. These core feelings create the *emotional architecture* of school climate, one that strengthens the capacity of all staff and students, supporting them through difficulties and enhancing their motivation to be successful. Within these core four feelings are subsets of related emotions and traits. For example, feeling safe encompasses related feelings of balance and calm. Feeling valued includes feeling satisfied and confident. To keep things streamlined, these four essential emotions are the core feelings that indicate a positive school climate and are the basis for this text.

The four core feelings are not accidental outcomes; they are intentionally cultivated through daily choices and consistent habits. The structure of this book mirrors the natural progression of these emotions, as each one builds on the last. Safety comes first, offering the steady ground from which all other feelings can grow. Support rises from that foundation, reminding individuals that they are not alone and giving them the structure and responsiveness needed to stay upright when challenges come. From this sense of steadiness and connection emerges the feeling of being valued—the importance of knowing that one's presence and contributions truly matter. And finally, when people feel safe, supported, and valued over time, fulfillment becomes possible. Fulfillment is the deeper sense of joy and purpose that sustains students and educators in the hardest moments and keeps them invested in the work.

Think of it this way: Safety enables support; support fosters feeling valued; feeling valued unlocks fulfillment.

These four feelings are interdependent; each strengthens the others. Remove one, and the climate becomes unbalanced. Nurture all four, and the school becomes a place where students and educators can thrive.

Who This Book Is For

We are in a moment of reckoning and reimagining. Educators are tired. Students are navigating layered realities. Our schools are being asked to do more than ever before. But here's what we believe: We do not need to work harder. We need to work *smarter*. We need to look upstream at the climate we're creating moment by moment and decision by decision. And we need tools that are grounded in research and easy to implement.

While much has been written about school culture, there are very few resources that specifically address *climate*. This book is for every educator who has felt the invisible weight of school climate without knowing exactly what to do to address it. It's for leaders who want to build strong foundations for those in their care. It's for teachers who want to change what's possible in their classrooms. It's for support staff who want to look forward to coming to work each day. It's for teams and districts that are ready to build schools where all humans thrive. It's for aspiring leaders seeking guidance as they prepare to embark on their leadership journey. It's for aspiring teachers studying to engage in one of the most meaningful professions on earth. We know that the work of cultivating transformational school climates doesn't belong to just one person or one role alone. Instead, it's a collective responsibility (Darling-Hammond, Schachner, & Edgerton, 2020). And it starts from the inside out.

In every school and in every classroom, every single day, we tend to the weather. As stated previously, some days the weather feels sunny and warm and full of connection, joy, and energy. On other days, it feels heavy and unsettled, like a storm is rolling in. The truth is, the emotional climate of our schools and classrooms is constantly shifting, but it's never out of our hands. As educators, we hold an incredible power: We can intentionally influence the way our environments feel, and this book shows you how to do it.

In this text, we refer to *adults* rather than specific job titles because this work involves everyone who works within a school. For us, *adults* means *all* the adults within the school community (administrators, teachers, paraprofessionals, aides, counselors, nurses, bus drivers, custodians, administrative assistants, speech pathologists, cafeteria staff, and so on) because every adult impacts school climate both through their work with other adults and with students. Therefore, we consider both adult-to-adult and adult-to-student strategies and incorporate potential student-to-student actions.

How to Use This Book

This work begins with a simple, transformative question: "How do I want the people in my care to feel today?" For some of you, that might mean asking, "How do I want my staff to feel as they return from winter break?" For others, it might mean asking, "How do I want my students to feel after they take today's assessment?" For others, it might mean, "How do I want my colleague to feel as she returns to work today after her maternity leave?"

We offer the four essential core feelings that define a positive school and classroom climate (shown in figure I.2) as the possible responses to the essential question, "How do I want the people in my care to feel today?"

At any point in the school day, whether on your way to work, during an off period, or as you're transitioning between tasks, you can pause and choose the feeling you most want to cultivate for those you serve (adults or students) in that moment or for that particular day. Additionally, we created a "Climate Chapter Diagnostic Tool" (see the appendix, page 146), which provides a quick guide to help you identify which core feeling needs your focus right now. Use this tool when you're unsure where to begin. Once you identify your desired feeling, simply turn to the corresponding chapter in this book for your next steps. Think of it like a

Source: OpenAI, 2025a.

Figure I.2: The four essential core feelings.

choose-your-own-adventure book. Each chapter is designed to meet you exactly where you are in that moment. Chapter 1 will aid your understanding of the four core feelings, the research that supports them, and the related feelings and traits that underpin them. In chapters 1–4, you'll find clear, easy-to-implement strategies that you can utilize immediately to attend to the feelings of adults *and* students as well as prompts you can plug into an AI tool for additional strategies tailored specifically to your environment.

For example:

- If you want those in your care to feel *safe*, in chapter 2, you'll find simple strategies to ensure a sense of order, enhance feelings of fairness, and affirm psychological security.
- If you want them to feel *supported*, in chapter 3, you'll discover ways to foster relationships, build trust within your community, and spark meaningful collaboration.
- If you want them to feel *valued*, in chapter 4, you'll uncover ideas for meaningful celebrations, recognition, and growth opportunities.
- If you are looking for *fulfillment*, in chapter 5, you'll find ways to reconnect to purpose, encourage autonomy, and move toward mastery.

Every strategy has been curated with the busy, committed educator in mind and designed to be practical, sustainable, and backed with research. You'll get to choose which strategy (or strategies) *you* want to implement to achieve the desired feeling you're seeking for those in your care. (You can find a full list of these strategies in the appendix, page 147.)

This text is meant to be used regularly; it's not a one-time read, nor is it a text that you read from front to back. It's a resource to be picked up again and again, perhaps even daily.

Consider this book as your first-aid kit. Tending to the daily climate of a school or classroom is, in many ways, a "Band-Aid" fix, an essential, immediate response to the emotional needs of the moment. It won't solve every systemic challenge overnight, nor will it replace the hard, ongoing work of building and sustaining a strong school culture. But just like a Band-Aid protects a wound so it can begin to heal, intentionally shaping the emotional climate each day creates the safety, trust, and stability needed for deeper transformation.

Another approach that school leaders may find helpful is to use this book for guiding professional learning and inspiring meaningful collaboration between team members during team meetings. Its structure is intentionally designed to promote purposeful dialogue among educators, inviting them to reflect on their own practices while connecting those reflections to the emotional and cultural dynamics of their teams and schools. Each chapter includes discussion prompts and practical strategies that can easily serve as the foundation for a structured cycle of professional learning, making this book a powerful resource not only for individual reflection but also for shared growth across a collaborative learning community.

You can find a "Simple Climate Implementation Protocol" in the appendix (page 150) to help put these practices into place. Using the four core feelings, this protocol is designed as a guide for educators to preplan, execute, and adjust a climate implementation plan for those in their care. This protocol provides support and guidance for all educators, whether teachers are planning effective classroom climates, campus administrators are planning effective school climates, or district leaders are planning effective district office climates.

> Climate work is where we start; self-care and educator wellness work provide the scaffolding, and school culture work is where we are heading.

No matter how you choose to work through this text, we also offer next steps that relate to self-care, educator wellness, and school culture because these three areas are deeply connected to one another. The goal is to eventually move from weather to season, from day-to-day emotional care (for ourselves and others) to a sustainable, thriving culture that holds steady no matter what storms may come. Climate work is where we start; self-care and educator wellness work provide the scaffolding, and school culture work is where we are heading.

Wherever you find yourself on your educational journey, we hope this book meets you with a hand on your back, a deep breath, and the encouragement to keep going. Together, we can create climates where every student and adult can flourish. Not *just* for a season, but for the long haul.

Let's begin!

CHAPTER 1

Understanding the Four Core Feelings

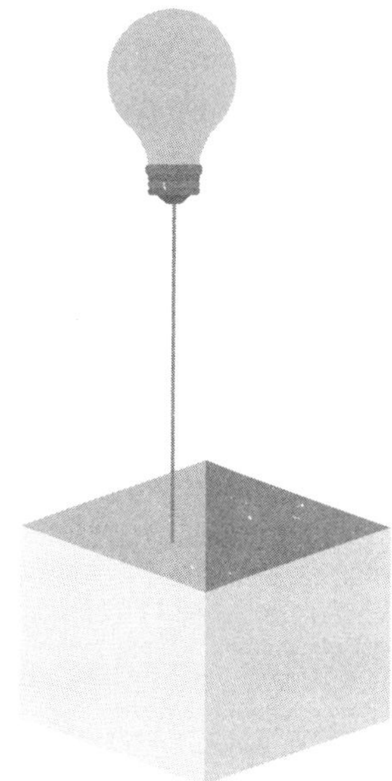

When school feels good, I can take a breath and actually learn instead of just bracing myself for the next hit.

—THIRD-GRADE STUDENT

When the climate is steady, I walk into my classroom ready to give my best instead of just trying to make it through the day.

—HIGH SCHOOL SCIENCE TEACHER

When the school climate is strong, I can spend my time developing people and not putting out fires.

—MIDDLE SCHOOL PRINCIPAL

We begin our journey with an invitation to step back and see the bigger picture. Before we begin exploring each feeling on its own, it's important to understand that the four core feelings—*safe*, *supported*, *valued*, and *fulfilled*—do not function as isolated experiences. Together, they form the *emotional architecture* of school climate, shaping how people think, behave, learn, and interact throughout the day. In this chapter, we introduce each of the four core feelings and break them down into specific sub-emotions or traits that make them visible in classrooms, hallways, staff rooms, team meetings, school buildings, and district offices. By understanding the building blocks of these feelings, we begin to see how strengthening one reinforces the others and creates the kind of climate where students and educators can flourish. (See the appendix, page 153, for a reproducible summarizing the four core feelings and their sub-emotions.)

First, we start with the most foundational feeling that allows all the others to take root: safety. Feeling safe is where everything begins. There's a reason we check the locks before we go to sleep. That quiet habit—the click of the deadbolt, the double-check of the garage—says something about our biology. We're hardwired to seek safety first. As educators, we sometimes overlook just how deep that need also runs in our schools. But the truth is, *nothing else matters until safety is in place.*

Feeling Safe

Safety isn't just the absence of physical harm; it's also the presence of emotional security.

Safety isn't just the absence of physical harm; it's also the presence of emotional security. It's the exhale we feel when we know we're OK, not only physically but also psychologically and socially. Safety isn't just about practicing fire and intruder drills; we also feel safe when our identity is respected or when a student is excited to come to school in the morning. All these moments are the building blocks of a school climate where adults and students thrive—when the weather feels sunny and warm.

Understanding the Landscape of Feeling Safe in Schools

Despite the significant strides we've made in school safety, the picture is still complex. Across the United States, schools have implemented stronger security protocols, including visitor sign-in systems, controlled access to school buildings, security cameras around campus, and active shooter drills (Irwin, Wang, Cui, & Thompson, 2024). Many schools also embrace proactive strategies like threat assessment frameworks and anonymous reporting systems like those supported by the official federal government site www.schoolsafety.gov, which provides resources and support for creating safer schools. Legislative efforts are evolving, too. For example, Connecticut passed laws refining crisis drills to prioritize both physical and psychological safety for students (Sokoloff, 2025).

And yet, we're still navigating persistent challenges. Multiple school shootings continue to occur each year (Rapa, Katsiyannis, Scott, & Durham, 2024), and bullying and mental health are also pressing concerns. Colorado's Safe2Tell program reports that 17.5 percent of its tips relate to bullying and 16.7 percent to mental health struggles (Colorado Office of the Attorney General, 2025). Additionally, schools face increasing threats to cybersecurity, with an average of five incidents reported weekly (U.S. Department of Education, 2025). In other words, while our efforts matter, keeping schools physically and emotionally safe is an ongoing, evolving commitment that requires both systems-level planning and deep human connection.

The discourse on school safety has expanded well beyond physical security measures to encompass emotional and psychological well-being. While much public attention has focused on school shootings and lockdown drills, educators and researchers alike recognize that true safety involves more than security. According to the National Center for Education Statistics (2023), about 69 percent of public schools reported an increase in students seeking mental health services during the 2021–2022 school year, and by 2023, 56 percent of public schools still reported higher levels of student need for mental health support compared with previous years, a clear indicator of the emotional strain students are experiencing. When emotional safety is compromised, students operate in survival mode—a state where their brains are focused on threat detection instead of learning (Immordino-Yang, Darling-Hammond, & Krone, 2019).

A Safety Story

At an elementary school tucked between busy streets and aging apartment complexes, nine-year-old Janelle used to drag her feet each morning, her stomach in knots from the unpredictability of home. But things started to shift when her new teacher, Ms. Carter, introduced a simple routine: Every student chose a starter task that felt just right for them. This could be drawing, reading, or writing in their journals. Janelle chose to draw and loved it. Each morning, Ms. Carter greeted her at the door with a warm smile and a gentle, "Your sketchbook is waiting for you." Over time, that predictability became her anchor. She knew exactly what to expect, and she knew someone was always glad she arrived. One day, she burst into the classroom early, ponytail swinging, saying, "I couldn't wait to show you my new picture!" Safety had opened the door to excitement. When students know they're protected, welcomed, and understood, school becomes a place they want to be, not a place they simply endure.

The Multifaceted Nature of Feeling Emotionally Safe

Safety in schools must be viewed through a comprehensive lens. The Collaborative for Academic, Social, and Emotional Learning (CASEL) emphasizes that emotional safety is built on key factors such as relational trust, cultural responsiveness, inclusive practices, and emotional regulation structures (Jagers, Rivas-Drake, & Borowski, 2018). These components are not add-ons; instead, they are the connective tissue of both effective instruction and school culture. For students, emotional safety means they can show up as their full selves without worrying about being laughed at, shut down, or punished for getting something wrong. It's knowing they can speak up, take risks, and make mistakes without it costing them connection or dignity. For adults in the building, it's about having the space to voice concerns, try new ideas, and receive honest feedback without fear of being criticized, dismissed, or penalized. Creating this type of environment requires strategic leadership, consistent communication, and shared norms around empathy, accountability, and repair.

What the Research Says About Emotionally Safe Schools

Studies suggest that emotionally safe environments are strongly correlated with academic success and student engagement, especially for students impacted by trauma. David Osher and Juliette Berg (2018) emphasize that when students feel emotionally and socially safe, they show improved executive function, better self-regulation, and stronger peer cooperation. Educators working in emotionally safe schools report greater job satisfaction and are less likely to leave the profession (Kraft, Marinell, & Yee, 2016). These findings reflect the critical role of emotional safety as both a prevention tool and a performance multiplier. Without it, no initiative, whether academic or behavioral, can take root.

Sub-Emotions and Traits That Signal Feeling Emotionally Safe

Research has consistently shown that emotional safety is layered and constructed from a foundation of distinct emotional experiences that signal psychological security. These sub-emotions and traits serve as internal cues that help students and staff navigate their surroundings. Because many of these emotions and traits are so vitally important, you will also see trust, respect, and inclusion as components of feeling valued.

1. **Trust:** Trust is a relational experience that grows when individuals perceive that those in authority respect them, listen to them, and act

with fairness and integrity. Relational trust is something that develops when students and staff believe that others have their best interests at heart, treat them with respect, communicate openly and honestly, follow through on commitments, and hold themselves accountable (Morrill & Musheno, 2018).

2. **Belonging:** Belonging is described as the experience of being accepted, valued, and included in the school community. It means that students and adults feel respected and seen for who they are, including their identities, cultures, and lived experiences. Belonging is not simply about being present in a space—it's about being *welcomed* and *affirmed* in that space (Hernández & Darling-Hammond, 2022).
3. **Respect:** Respect means perceiving that you are treated with dignity and fairness. Respect is not just about courtesy—it's about deep acknowledgment of a person's identity and ideas. When respect is present, classrooms and staff meetings become spaces where people feel brave enough to speak up (Mokracek & Mohammed, 2022).
4. **Predictability:** Predictability is feeling grounded in clear expectations and consistent routines. It doesn't mean rigidity; it means reliability. In safe schools, students know what will happen next (Pierantoni, 2017). Staff members are not surprised by policy changes or shifts in expectations. Predictable systems lower stress and create mental space for creativity and engagement (Dunavete, 2024).
5. **Inclusion:** Inclusion is the experience of being intentionally welcomed, regardless of background or identity (Jardinez & Natividad, 2024). It extends beyond diversity to ensure every individual feels welcome and valued. Without it, emotional isolation grows, particularly for those from historically marginalized communities.
6. **Calm:** Calm is the ability to stay emotionally grounded and free from overwhelm (Jennings, 2019). Calm isn't the absence of energy; it's the ability to channel emotion in healthy, constructive ways. Emotionally safe environments teach and model self-regulation strategies, offering all stakeholders tools to stay composed and focused, even under stress.

Together, these six sub-emotions and traits don't just support the academic mission, they *enable* it; they shape how teachers teach, how leaders lead, and how students learn.

Figure 1.1 (page 22) summarizes these findings for quick reference.

Sub-Emotions and Traits	Definition	Why It Matters
Trust	A relational experience that grows when individuals perceive that those in authority respect them, listen to them, and act with fairness and integrity	Trust is essential in schools because it fosters psychological safety, encourages collaboration, supports conflict resolution, and strengthens behavioral expectations, all of which contribute to a safe and supportive environment for students and staff.
Belonging	The feeling of being accepted and valued by a group	Belonging reduces fear of exclusion, which is critical for emotional safety.
Respect	The perception of being treated with dignity, fairness, and consideration	Respectful treatment minimizes fear of humiliation or rejection.
Predictability	The sense that routines, norms, and expectations are consistent and reliable	Predictability reduces anxiety and helps individuals anticipate outcomes.
Inclusion	The feeling of being invited, considered, and valued, regardless of identity or background	Inclusion prevents marginalization and fosters a climate of acceptance.
Calm	The emotional state of feeling grounded and free from threat or overwhelming stress	A regulated emotional climate supports safe learning and working conditions.

Figure 1.1: Sub-emotions and traits related to feeling emotionally safe.
*Visit **go.SolutionTree.com/schoolimprovement** for a free reproducible version of this figure.*

Turn to chapter 2 to learn how to ensure those in your care feel emotionally safe.

Feeling Supported

We can all remember a time when someone believed in us before we believed in ourselves. Perhaps it was a colleague who nudged us forward, a mentor who made space when we needed it, or a friend who listened, really listened, without trying to fix us. These are not just moments of kindness; they're the scaffolding that holds us up when we're learning, stretching, or starting to doubt ourselves. In schools, feeling supported is a powerful internal signal that tells us we're not alone. Once we're safe, feeling supported allows us to stretch ourselves. Just like safety, support is a prerequisite to feeling both valued and fulfilled. Without support, confidence falters, motivation evaporates, and disconnection takes root (Ryan & Deci, 2020). But with it, the climate changes in a positive way; people try harder, reach farther, and believe more, both in themselves and in one another (Jolly, Kong, & Kim, 2021).

Understanding the Landscape of Feeling Supported in Schools

In the current educational climate, demands on students and staff continue to climb (Gallup, 2023). Educators are asked to do more with less, manage complex student needs, implement new initiatives, and respond to rising mental health concerns, all while trying to stay afloat themselves. Students, too, face mounting pressures, such as academic rigor, social expectations, and trauma exposure, often within environments that lack responsive support systems.

According to university professors and researchers in the field of clinical psychology Baiba Martinsone, Sergio Di Sano, Paola D'Elia, and Tamika La Salle-Finley (2023), schools that intentionally build supportive climates report stronger engagement, greater resilience, and reduced burnout for both staff and students. When people feel supported, they're more likely to take academic and professional risks, maintain their well-being, and recover from setbacks.

> Feeling supported requires a responsive ecosystem where encouragement is offered, resources are accessible, and someone has your back.

While it's tempting to think of support as just good interpersonal behavior, it's far more than that. Feeling supported requires a responsive ecosystem where encouragement is offered, resources are accessible, and someone has your back. (Zhang & Luo, 2023). It's about care, yes, but feeling supported is also about access, responsiveness, and shared investment. When that system is in place, individuals begin to feel anchored rather than adrift.

A Support Story

At a newcomer academy housed within an urban middle school, a seventh grader named Ahmed had arrived only three months earlier from Sudan. English still felt like a maze to him, full of turns he couldn't see coming or understand. One afternoon, while students were working on a collaborative science project, his teacher quietly pulled up a chair beside him and translated the directions using simple visuals they had built together. She didn't rush him and didn't hover; she just stayed close enough, so he knew he wasn't navigating the task alone. Afterward, he whispered, "Thank you for helping me." For students building a new life in a new language, support is not just helpful; it is a lifeline.

The Multifaceted Nature of Feeling Supported

Support is not a single interaction; it's a layered experience that communicates that someone else sees you, believes in you, and will show up for you. While care is central to support, so is action. Encouragement without access can feel hollow, and responsiveness without advocacy can feel performative; true support is comprehensive.

For students, feeling supported means knowing there's someone who will notice when they're struggling and do something about it. It means having access to help without stigma or delay. Support is the difference between success and failure, between isolation or inclusion. For adults, it means not having to pretend everything's fine when it's not. It's knowing your voice matters, your needs count, and someone will step in if you're sinking. Support can be the difference between endurance and burnout.

What the Research Says About Supportive School Environments

Support is a powerful predictor of engagement, retention, and resilience in school communities. A comprehensive study conducted by the U.S. Department of Education (2021) finds that encouragement significantly boosts persistence and reduces isolation, especially in high-stress environments. Further, mentorship, which is a relational form of sustained support, improves belonging, confidence, and academic identity (Ravishankar et al., 2024). Jelena Veletić, Heather E. Price, and Rolf Vegar Olsen (2023) state that responsiveness, particularly in leadership and teaching, builds emotional trust and deepens school climate. Support isn't soft; instead, it's strategic, and its presence often distinguishes thriving schools from merely surviving ones.

Sub-Emotions and Traits That Signal Feeling Supported

Support is not a singular emotion but a constellation of experiences. It is built through repeated moments that signal to someone that they are not navigating challenges alone. Support emerges when encouragement is paired with access and when guidance is available as needed. People feel supported when they know someone will notice if they need help. Over time, these experiences combine to create the steady belief that assistance is both present and reliable.

1. **Encouragement:** Encouragement is the felt experience of someone believing in your potential—even when you're unsure of it yourself. In schools, students feel encouraged when teachers recognize their efforts, not just their outcomes, and nudge them to try again after setbacks. For adults, encouragement may show up as a colleague validating an idea during a meeting or a school leader expressing confidence in their capacity to lead change. When encouragement is consistently present, it helps build persistence and resilience in both students and staff, particularly during moments of challenge or self-doubt (Collins et al., 2024).
2. **Accessibility:** Accessibility refers to the ability to reach people, resources, or support without barriers. For students, this might look like knowing a counselor is available without having to jump through hoops or that accommodations are implemented smoothly. For adults, it could mean having access to planning time, coaching, or even mental health resources without stigma. When help feels close and easy to reach, people are more likely to trust their environment and are less likely to feel overwhelmed (Ruzek, 2025).
3. **Responsiveness:** Responsiveness is the sense that when someone expresses a need, someone else listens—and does something about it. For students, this might mean a teacher noticing when they're disengaged and gently checking in or adjusting expectations to reduce stress. For adults, responsiveness may be a principal acting on staff feedback or adjusting a policy that's causing unintended harm. When people feel heard and see action, it builds trust and signals that they are not alone in solving problems (Dirks & de Jong, 2022).
4. **Mentorship:** Mentorship is the presence of a consistent, trusted guide—someone who offers advice, listens, and models the path ahead. Students experience mentorship when a teacher or older peer consistently checks in on their goals or provides guidance on both

academic and personal decisions. Adults benefit from mentorship through instructional coaching, leadership pipelines, or informal relationships that offer perspective and encouragement. In both cases, mentorship supports confidence, skill growth, and a sense of belonging (Ravishankar et al., 2024).

5. **Advocacy:** Advocacy is the belief that someone will stand up for you when it matters. For students, this might mean a teacher intervening when they're being treated unfairly or recommending them for an opportunity they didn't know existed. For adults, advocacy looks like a leader protecting planning time, defending staff against undue criticism, or amplifying their ideas in decision-making spaces. Advocacy is support in action. It reinforces the idea that people matter beyond just their productivity (Mohan et al., 2024).

Together, these five sub-emotions and traits shape the emotional infrastructure of support. Their presence is felt in daily decisions, such as when a leader offers help without asking, acknowledges ideas, or removes barriers rather than ignoring them.

Figure 1.2 provides a summary of the key sub-emotions and traits that shape the internal feeling of being supported.

Sub-Emotion	Definition	Why It Matters
Encouragement	The experience of being uplifted by others who believe in one's abilities	Fosters persistence and resilience, especially in challenging learning or work situations (Hecht, Bryan, & Yeager, 2023)
Accessibility	Knowing that help, tools, or people are available when needed	Promotes confidence and reduces stress by assuring reliable support systems (Skaalvik & Skaalvik, 2020)
Responsiveness	The sense that others listen, understand, and act on one's needs	Builds emotional safety and trust in leadership or instruction (Dedering & Pietsch, 2025)
Mentorship	Having trusted adults or peers who guide, advise, and advocate	Promotes skill development, emotional well-being, and belonging (Bambrick-Santoyo, 2025)

Sub-Emotion	Definition	Why It Matters
Advocacy	Feeling that someone is actively championing one's needs or rights	Protects against marginalization and builds a culture that prioritizes inclusion (Theoharis, 2024)

Figure 1.2: Sub-emotions and traits related to feeling supported.

*Visit **go.SolutionTree.com/schoolimprovement** for a free reproducible version of this figure.*

Turn to chapter 3 to learn how to ensure those in your care feel supported.

Feeling Valued

There's something powerful about hearing, "I'm glad you're here." It doesn't require time or money; it's just a few intentional words that say, "You matter." In schools, the emotional climate often hinges on whether people feel seen. When students and adults feel truly valued, not just tolerated or managed, it changes how they show up.

Feeling valued isn't about flattery or surface-level rewards. Instead, it's about a deeper affirmation: *You are important here*. That message, whether conveyed through a morning greeting or deliberately announced in a team celebration, is one of the most effective levers we have for improving school climate.

When we don't feel valued, we might withdraw, go quiet, and disengage. In schools, that disconnection isn't just a private matter; it shows up in attendance, behavior, relationships, and achievement. But when feeling valued *is* present, the entire school becomes warmer, more vibrant, and more resilient.

Understanding the Landscape of Feeling Valued in Schools

Despite growing awareness around the importance of school climate, far too many students and educators across the United States still report feeling invisible. In a nationwide survey of over 66,000 secondary students, only 46 percent said they felt like valued members of their school community (DeWitt, 2016). That number is more than a statistic—it's a wake-up call.

Despite growing awareness around the importance of school climate, far too many students and educators across the United States still report feeling invisible.

Research consistently links feeling valued to tangible benefits. Students who report feeling valued by their peers and teachers have better attendance, higher grades, stronger mental health, and fewer behavioral issues (Balfanz, Jerabek, Payne, & Scala, 2024; Centers for Disease Control and Prevention [CDC], 2024). Educators, too, are more likely to stay in their roles, collaborate meaningfully, and show up with energy when they feel their voices and contributions matter (Ball, 2025).

Being valued is both a personal experience and a shared one. When one student feels seen, they ripple that energy out to others. When a teacher feels heard by their principal, that respect flows into how they treat their students. In this way, valuing others becomes a collective act, a practice that strengthens the emotional fabric of a school.

A Value Story

At a suburban high school, Mr. Alvarez taught eleventh-grade English. He poured himself into crafting discussions that mattered, curated readings that connected to students' real lives, and stayed late most evenings to help students revise essays or just talk. Still, he often wondered if any of it made a difference. Then, during the spring pep assembly, something unexpected happened. After the marching band marched off and the cheer squad finished their routine, the student council president stepped up to the mic and said, "This year, we created a new student-voted award: The Teacher Who Sees You." The gym buzzed, and she continued, "And the person who received the most nominations is . . . Mr. Alvarez." The students erupted in cheers!

As Mr. Alvarez walked to center court, stunned, a senior handed him a poster with thank-you notes from all his students and whispered, "You make this school feel different." In that moment, Mr. Alvarez didn't just feel appreciated. It was deeper than that: He felt *valued*. His influence wasn't invisible after all; it was woven into the very fabric of the school community.

The Multifaceted Nature of Feeling Valued

Feeling valued is built on everyday interactions: a teacher who calls students by name, a principal who invites staff input, or a class project that honors student identity. All these actions communicate the belief that everyone in the school is valued.

Linda Darling-Hammond and Channa M. Cook-Harvey (2018) explain that affirming a student's value and competence can lead to marked improvements in test scores and emotional well-being. Similarly, when teachers feel recognized and trusted by leadership, their morale and instructional effectiveness all rise, and they are more likely to stay (Grissom, Egalite, & Lindsay, 2021).

Significantly, the experience of being valued must extend to *all* members of the school community. This includes students from marginalized backgrounds, support staff who are often overlooked, and veteran teachers whose contributions can become expected rather than celebrated. As Caitlynn Peetz Stephens and Laura Baker (2024) note, even the bus driver who knows students' names is shaping school climate by showing others that they matter.

What the Research Says About Feeling Valued in Schools

Data from EdResearch for Action (Balfanz et al., 2024) shows that students who feel valued by peers and adults in the building attend school more regularly, achieve more academically, and report stronger mental health.

For educators, feeling valued is tightly linked to staying power. In a 2024 study, Matthew A. Kraft and Melissa Arnold Lyon find that when teachers feel respected and included in decision making, they are far more likely to remain in the profession (Ball, 2025). Trust in leadership and acknowledgment of effort, alongside a collaborative environment, all signal: *You are needed here.* A Wallace Foundation report by Jason A. Grissom, Anna J. Egalite, and Constance A. Lindsay (2021) emphasizes that principals who actively work to ensure students and staff feel emotionally supported and valued create healthier, more successful schools.

Sub-Emotions and Traits That Signal Feeling Valued

Just as safety and support are layered, so is the experience of feeling valued. The following are six emotional indicators, or sub-emotions or traits, that signal to someone: *You matter here.* You may notice some overlay of the essential emotions or traits included in feeling safe—trust, inclusion, and respect—as these are essential for both.

1. **Recognition:** Recognition is the feeling that your efforts are noticed and your presence is acknowledged. For students, this might mean a teacher praises their hard work. For adults, it might be a leader who follows up on an idea mentioned in passing. Recognition affirms we are not invisible.

2. **Inclusion:** Inclusion means being invited in. One isn't just allowed to be present; they are welcomed and integrated. Inclusion happens when students' cultures are reflected in the curriculum, students have access to diverse educators, paraprofessionals are part of staff celebrations, and all voices have a seat at the table.
3. **Respect:** Respect involves being treated with dignity and fairness, especially during moments of conflict or challenge. When people feel respected, even in disagreement, they feel valued. It's the difference between being dismissed and being considered.
4. **Support:** Support is the experience of knowing someone has your back. That might be a colleague covering a duty or task, a mentor offering feedback, or a student receiving extra help without shame. Support says: *I believe in you, and I'm here.*
5. **Trust:** Trust grows when we feel that others see us as competent and honest and when we feel safe to be ourselves. When we're trusted, we are more likely to contribute and take risks.
6. **Appreciation:** Appreciation is the expression of gratitude for who we are and what we offer—not just for results, but also for effort and attitude. It sounds like: *Thanks for being here* and *You make a difference.*

Figure 1.3 summarizes these findings for quick reference.

Sub-Emotion	Definition	Why It Matters
Recognition	Feeling seen and acknowledged for one's contributions or presence	Recognition boosts self-worth and strengthens motivation.
Inclusion	Being invited and welcomed into decision making, conversation, and community	Inclusion prevents emotional isolation and affirms belonging.
Respect	Being treated with dignity, fairness, and regard	Respect creates safety, especially in moments of disagreement.
Support	Knowing others will offer help or stand beside you when needed	Support builds resilience and relational trust.

Sub-Emotion	Definition	Why It Matters
Trust	Being believed in and granted responsibility or autonomy	Trust encourages deeper engagement and authentic participation.
Appreciation	Feeling that your presence and contributions are valued	Appreciation affirms that you matter just as you are.

Figure 1.3: Sub-emotions and traits related to feeling valued.

*Visit **go.SolutionTree.com/schoolimprovement** for a free reproducible version of this figure.*

Turn to chapter 4 to learn how to ensure those in your care feel valued.

Feeling Fulfilled

There's a unique satisfaction that comes from stepping back and realizing you are happy with what you are doing. It's not quick satisfaction from ticking off tasks but a lasting sense that your work is meaningful. Feeling fulfilled is the quiet confidence that you're on a path worth traveling, your contributions matter, and you are becoming more capable along the way (Baumann & Ruch, 2022). In schools, fulfillment is what sustains people through their inevitable challenges (Wang, Yang, Chen, & Zheng, 2023). It's what keeps students leaning into hard work and educators returning with renewed resolve and determination to ensure the success of each of their students year after year.

When fulfillment is present, individuals take pride in their progress and feel confident in their ability to be successful (Koivunen, Pyöriä, & Saari, 2023). On the other hand, when fulfillment is absent, students and staff can drift into apathy and disengagement and recoil during challenging moments. Fulfillment is an essential emotional anchor that shapes how people engage, persist, and excel in their work (Moreno, 2023).

Understanding the Landscape of Feeling Fulfilled in Schools

Schools operate in a high-demand, high-accountability, and potentially burnout-inducing climate where achievement is often measured in test scores, surface-level performance measures, politically driven outcomes, and top-down compliance measures. Yet research shows that a sense of fulfillment will not develop in climates focused on top-down, rigid accountability. Instead, true motivation and engagement are rooted in climates that foster purpose, autonomy, pride, joy, and progress (Engels,

Spilt, Denies, & Verschueren, 2021; Ryan & Deci, 2017). In a school with a regularly positive climate, these feelings are intentionally prioritized and supported. Feelings of fulfillment should be systematically cultivated in classrooms, schools, and districts.

For students, fulfillment emerges when they see their learning as meaningful—when they understand what they are being asked to learn, connect the tasks they are assigned to achievable learning outcomes, feel trusted to make learning decisions, can track and experience growth, and take pride in their accomplishments. For educators, it's the sense that their work is aligned with their values, their professional judgment matters, their students are motivated and engaged, they see tangible success in their students, and their success as an educator is both noticed and celebrated.

When schools cultivate these experiences, they create climates where people approach their days with passion and desire to be the best version of themselves. Conversely, the absence of fulfillment is costly. Without purpose, motivation erodes. Without autonomy, creativity stalls. Without pride, self-worth diminishes. Without joy, energy wanes. Without progress, confidence falters. Over time, these gaps contribute to disengagement, resistance, and a decline in overall school climate (Moreno, 2023; Sharma, Gupta, & Verma, 2025).

A Fulfillment Story

At a rural middle school, assistant principal Dana Collins often joked that her job was equal parts leader, counselor, air-traffic controller, and firefighter. Her days were a blur of discipline referrals, parent meetings, and trying to keep a dozen spinning plates from crashing to the floor. She loved her school, but lately, she'd been wondering if any of her work truly made a difference, or if she was simply patching holes in a ship taking on water.

Then came the eighth-grade passion projects showcase. Dana had supported the teachers in designing the unit months earlier by helping them map out timelines, secure community mentors, and carve out space in a jam-packed schedule. She wasn't sure if all that effort had landed the way they'd hoped.

But as she walked into the gym that evening, she stopped short. Students were beaming beside trifold boards, prototypes, videos, and handmade creations. Parents and community members leaned in, genuinely engaged; teachers floated around the room, proud and animated; and everywhere Dana turned, someone waved her over, saying, "You have to see this one!" "Ms. Collins, come check this out!" A student named Laila tugged on her sleeve and said shyly, "I made a podcast about being a first-generation kid. You're the one who encouraged me to share my story." By the end of the night, Dana stood near the exit and watched families stream out, laughing and carrying projects with them. A quiet warmth washed over her with a steady sense of, *This is why I do it.*

For the first time in months, she felt deeply fulfilled, not because the day had been easy, but because she could see the cumulative impact of her work. She helped created the conditions for teachers to thrive and students to shine.

The Multifaceted Nature of Feeling Fulfilled

Fulfillment is not a single emotion but is instead a cumulative effect of multiple reinforcing experiences. Each one shapes how we perceive our work, our learning, and ourselves. In schools, these experiences can be intentionally designed into daily practice.

For example, purpose can be nurtured when a student's work contributes to something beyond themselves, such as creating resources for younger classmates or leading a project that improves their community (Damon, Menon, & Bronk, 2019). Likewise, a feeling of purpose can manifest when an educator's professional learning is aligned with their passions (Collie, & Martin, 2017). Autonomy can be strengthened when students have choices in how they demonstrate mastery and teachers have flexibility in instructional design (Reeve, & Cheon, 2021). Pride grows when achievements, both large and small, are acknowledged and celebrated (Kosfeld, Neckermann, & Yang, 2017). Joy emerges in classrooms and staffrooms where curiosity and connection are part of the daily lived experiences for educators and their students (Martinsone, Di Sano, D'Elia, & La Salle-Finley, 2023). Progress allows growth to be visible for both students and educators when feedback is timely, specific, constructive, and improvement focused (Hattie & Clarke, 2018). Fulfillment thrives in environments where these elements are not accidental but intentional (Seligman, 2018).

What the Research Says About Feeling Fulfilled in Schools

The research base underscores that fulfillment is a powerful driver of performance and well-being. Feeling fulfilled does more than make the workday more pleasant; it fundamentally changes how people approach their work. When people feel fulfilled in work and learning, both long-term motivation and resilience are enhanced and productivity rises because individuals bring more energy, focus, and creativity to the tasks in front of them (Kashdan, Goodman, McKnight, Brown, & Rum, 2024). Fulfillment also drives success by creating a positive feedback loop. The more people feel that their contributions matter, the more they invest; the more they invest, the stronger their outcomes (Pincus, 2023).

Equally important, fulfillment fosters satisfaction and well-being. People who feel fulfilled are less likely to burn out because their work is energizing rather than draining (Fernet, Morin, Mueller, Gillet, & Austin, 2023). They experience a sense of balance, knowing that their time and effort contribute to something larger than themselves. This satisfaction strengthens retention for educators and resilience for students, creating stability in classrooms and across entire schools. Fulfillment, in other words, allows people to feel accomplished and connected to something bigger than their own work, both individually and collectively.

Sub-Emotions and Traits That Signal Feeling Fulfilled

Fulfillment is not a single feeling but a collection of five core sub-emotions or traits: (1) purpose, (2) autonomy, (3) joy, (4) pride, and (5) progress. Each plays a vital role in shaping how students and educators experience meaning in their daily lives at school. Together, they form the emotional foundation that keeps people energized, resilient, focused, creative, committed to growth, and connected to outcomes bigger than themselves.

1. **Purpose:** The first sub-emotion, *purpose*, is the anchor. Purpose is what tells us that our work matters; it is the belief that what we do has meaning beyond the task itself (Herr, Brokmeier, Baron, Mauss, & Fischer, 2023). When students and educators feel a strong sense of purpose, it transforms routine tasks into meaningful contributions and turns effort into an investment worth making because the effort impacts something bigger than their individual work (Sharma, Yukhymenko-Lescroart, & Sanchez, 2023).

2. **Autonomy:** Autonomy functions as a powerful companion to purpose; it fosters innovation, deepens engagement, and strengthens intrinsic motivation (Ryan & Deci, 2017). Autonomy gives fulfillment its shape. It is the experience of being trusted to make choices and to direct one's own path. Autonomy strengthens voice and agency, reminding both students and educators that their decisions matter (Patzak & Zhang, 2025). It transforms compliance into commitment and creates conditions where creativity and confidence can thrive. Autonomy also cultivates ownership, reinforcing the idea that progress and success are not simply handed down but actively created through one's own choices and actions.
3. **Joy:** Joy is the spark of fulfillment. It is the emotional lift that makes the hard work of learning and educating feel worth it. Joy contributes to mental health, reduces burnout risk, and sustains energy over time (Cronqvist, 2024). Joy is the emotional spark that makes the work of teaching and learning come alive.
4. **Pride:** Just like with joy, pride is an essential part of feeling fulfilled because it reinforces identity and commitment and encourages individuals to maintain high standards (Vijai, 2025). Pride is the affirmation of fulfillment and the deep satisfaction that comes from effort meeting achievement (Tracy, Mercadante, & Hohm, 2023).
5. **Progress:** Progress is the momentum of fulfillment. It is the recognition that growth is happening by taking small, steady steps or transformative leaps. Progress assures students and educators that their efforts are not in vain. Progress is the feeling of forward movement and growth. Feeling fulfilled can have a powerful impact on school climate when students and educators see the tangible results of their efforts and feel a deeper sense of purpose, autonomy, joy, pride, and progress.

These sub-emotions and traits foster and sustain fulfillment. Together, they act as signposts that indicate how someone's work or learning is aligned with personal meaning, agency, happiness, affirmation, and growth. Fostering and supporting these sub-emotions and traits is critical to sustaining a thriving school climate.

Figure 1.4 (page 36) summarizes these findings for quick reference.

Sub-Emotion	Definition	Why It Matters
Purpose	A sense that one's work or learning has meaning and impact	Increases motivation and effort, improving performance; strengthens long-term resilience; and reduces burnout increasing job satisfaction
Autonomy	Feeling empowered to make decisions and direct one's actions	Enhances voice and ownership, fosters innovation and intrinsic motivation, and increases employee retention
Joy	A genuine emotional response of happiness and satisfaction	Encourages risk-taking, increases camaraderie, fosters celebration, and encourages new efforts and ideas
Pride	Internal satisfaction with effort, growth, or success	Produces affirmation of efforts, reinforces identity and commitment, encourages self-imposed high expectations, encourages resilience, and increases satisfaction
Progress	The experience of tangible growth or improvement over time	Builds efficacy and positive momentum, increases competence and confidence, fosters innovation, encourages persistence, and increases one's belief in their ability to be successful

Figure 1.4: Sub-emotions and traits related to feeling fulfilled.

*Visit **go.SolutionTree.com/schoolimprovement** for a free reproducible version of this figure.*

Turn to chapter 5 to learn how to ensure those in your care feel fulfilled.

Conclusion

At the heart of every school community lies a set of emotional currents that shape how people feel and interact with one another and their work. In this chapter, we explored four essential feelings: safe, supported, valued, and fulfilled. Together, these feelings form the emotional foundation of a healthy school climate. We presented these core feelings not as abstract ideals, but rather as lived experiences that shape whether schools feel like places of possibility or places of survival. When these feelings are consistently present, they transform climate into culture and weave connection, trust, and purpose into the very fabric of the school. When absent, the entire system falters.

The implications for school climate are profound. A student who feels safe is more likely to take academic risks. A teacher who feels supported is more willing to innovate. A staff member who feels valued is more likely to remain engaged and committed. A community that feels fulfilled approaches challenges with confidence and hope rather than fatigue and resignation. These feelings are not simply nice to have; they are essential conditions for learning, teaching, and leading.

Recognizing the importance of these feelings is only the beginning. The real work lies in intentionally creating the conditions in which they can flourish. School climate is not accidental; instead, effective school climates are cultivated through choices, habits, and systems. That is why the chapters that follow move from understanding to action. Each chapter provides practical strategies for nurturing these core feelings at every level of the educational system.

School climate is not accidental; instead, effective school climates are cultivated through choices, habits, and systems.

For teachers, the following chapters offer concrete classroom practices to ensure students consistently feel safe, supported, valued, and fulfilled. You will find strategies for designing actions and routines that build the conditions for each of the four core feelings for the students in your care.

For schools, the chapters ahead outline leadership practices that strengthen staff climate. These include ways to design systems and structures that foster a climate centered on safety, support, value, and fulfillment for all members of a school staff.

For districts, the chapters elevate system-level strategies to sustain these core feelings across schools. This includes policies that prioritize emotional safety alongside physical security, structures that provide ongoing mentorship and development for staff, communication practices that affirm value at every level, and accountability systems that measure not only outcomes but also the climate conditions that drive them.

Each of these levels—classroom, school, and district—plays a critical role in cultivating the emotional stability of a community. When aligned, they create a climate where the four core feelings are not occasional sparks but enduring patterns. And when these patterns are consistent, they evolve into school culture and form the deep, lasting character of a school that outlives initiatives, survives leadership changes, and continues to shape how people feel for years to come.

The promise of the four core feelings is clear: Schools can become places where students and educators alike feel safe enough to take risks, supported enough to persist, valued enough to contribute, and fulfilled enough to thrive. The work ahead is not simple, but it is possible, and it is vital for successful schools.

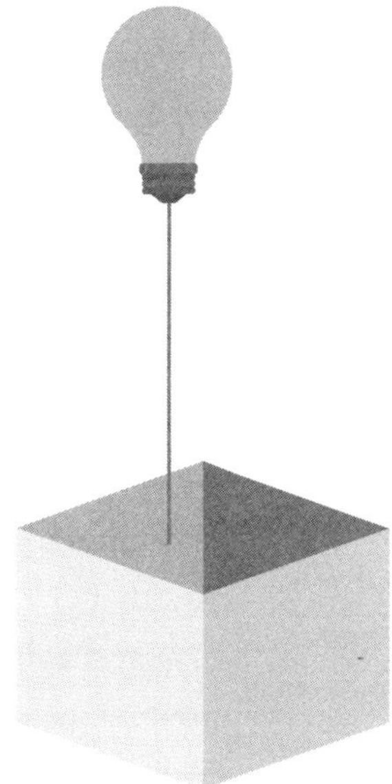

CHAPTER 2

Feeling Safe

When I don't feel safe, every single thing feels like a threat, even the stuff that shouldn't.
—ELEVENTH-GRADE STUDENT

When I don't feel safe emotionally, I stop taking risks, stop sharing ideas, and just try to make it through the day.
—KINDERGARTEN TEACHER

When safety slips, the whole building tightens, and every decision feels like it might break something instead of build something.
—HIGH SCHOOL PRINCIPAL

You're here because you care deeply. You want your school, your classroom, your team, your hallway, and even your meetings to feel safe. Not just safe from physical harm, but emotionally safe as well. You want the people in your care—students, colleagues, and staff members—to be able to exhale, unclench their jaws, relax their shoulders, and experience that quiet, reassuring sense of *I am safe here.*

That kind of safety changes everything. When people feel safe, their nervous systems settle. They think more clearly, listen more openly, and engage more fully. They are more willing to ask questions, try new strategies, admit mistakes, and grow. Without safety, learning and collaboration become much harder. With it, people begin to show up as their full selves.

Here is the good news: Safety is not out of reach. It is not theoretical, and it is not reserved for a small group of experts. While administrators, counselors, and specialists play essential roles, creating physical and emotional safety is ultimately the work of an entire community. It lives in everyday actions—in the tone of our voices, the predictability of our routines, the way we respond when someone makes a mistake, and the signals we send about whether people are truly welcome and respected.

In this chapter, we explore practical, research-based strategies to strengthen both physical and emotional safety in two vital areas: between adults and between adults and students. These strategies are intentionally simple and sustainable. They are not grand initiatives or complicated programs. Instead, they are small, consistent practices that gradually build trust and stability one interaction at a time. Whether you serve at the district level, teach in a classroom, lead a campus, or work in a role that often happens behind the scenes, this chapter invites you into the quiet, powerful work of creating safety. Because people only grow—academically, professionally, and personally—when they feel safe enough to do so.

You Might Need This Chapter If . . .

You might need this chapter if you're finding that people are operating in a constant state of tension. If your staff meetings feel heavy and guarded, if your students scan the room before they speak, or if you've felt the silence that follows a tough moment, you're in the right place. You might have noticed more withdrawn body language, shorter tempers, or the quiet resignation of students who have stopped raising their hands in class or staff asking for help at work. These are climate cues. They don't always scream; sometimes they whisper. But they all point to a fundamental need that isn't being met: the need to feel safe.

Before diving into the strategies ahead, take a moment to check in with what's happening around you. Safety is the foundation of everything in your climate. If emotional or physical safety is shaky, even slightly, every other feeling becomes harder to grow.

Safety is the foundation of everything in your climate. If emotional or physical safety is shaky, even slightly, every other feeling becomes harder to grow.

To perform a quick diagnostic check, use the following questions to help you discern whether safety is the area calling for your attention. (You can find the "Climate Chapter Diagnostic Tool" in the appendix, page 146.)

- Are students or adults hesitant to speak because they're unsure if their words are welcome?
- Have you noticed withdrawal, guardedness, or silence replacing participation?
- Do people brace for correction or conflict instead of trusting they'll be treated with dignity?
- Are routines or expectations inconsistent enough to make people anxious or uncertain?
- Do tensions, even small ones, seem to shape how people move through the halls, enter classrooms, or show up to meetings?

If you can answer *yes* to most of these questions, start here. Safety is the soil from which every other feeling grows. We offer immediate safety strategies and ideas for strategy design for both adult-to-adult and adult-to-student situations. If you have read this chapter before and understand the emotions and traits associated with the need to feel safe, you may choose to proceed straight to the strategy sections.

When People Don't Feel Emotionally Safe

To help understand how these emotions show up in schools and classrooms, let's examine the emotions and traits that arise when each of the sub-emotions or traits is missing. Figure 2.1 is a summary of these findings. (You can find a list of all the sub-emotions related to the four core feelings in the appendix, page 153.)

Missing Sub-Emotion or Trait	Common Emotions Experienced	Why These Emotions Arise
Trust	Fear, suspicion, anxiety, insecurity	Loss of psychological safety and fear of betrayal or harm cause people to withdraw from one another and protect themselves rather than participate fully.
Belonging	Loneliness, shame, rejection, depression	Social exclusion triggers emotional pain and a loss of connection that can begin eroding how people show up, leading to withdrawal, disengagement, or protection from further rejection.

Figure 2.1: Emotional impact when people don't feel emotionally safe.

continued ▶

Respect	Embarrassment, anger, worthlessness, resentment	Threats to dignity and perceived worth provoke distress and defense, often shifting people into a posture of self-protection rather than engagement.
Predictability	Confusion, anxiety, helplessness, frustration	Inconsistency and lack of control cause cognitive and emotional strain, forcing people to spend more energy managing uncertainty than engaging in their work.
Inclusion	Shame, alienation, jealousy, sadness	Exclusion based on identity disrupts self-worth and social belonging, sending a powerful signal that a person's full self is not welcomed in the community.
Calm	Overwhelm, irritability, panic, rage, shutdown	Lack of regulation limits coping and increases emotional volatility, making it harder for individuals to respond thoughtfully when challenges arise.

Visit ***go.SolutionTree.com/schoolimprovement*** *for a free reproducible version of this figure.*

It's important to remember: The absence of safety impacts both adults and students.

When Adults Don't Feel Emotionally Safe

When the sub-emotions of safety are absent, adults don't simply notice a gap; they feel it deeply, often in ways that disrupt their work and overall well-being. A lack of trust can lead to fear and anxiety. Educators may feel like they are constantly on edge, second-guess colleagues or administrators, and brace for criticism rather than engage in collaborative conversations. Without belonging, adults can feel isolated and reluctant to contribute to staff meetings or team discussions. When respect is missing, embarrassment and resentment brew, especially if staff feel dismissed or unheard (Hoffman, 2023).

Unpredictable environments, like those with unclear expectations or shifting priorities, result in confusion and chronic stress or anxiety. Adults may describe their workplace as "chaotic" or "constantly changing," which diminishes their confidence and morale (American Psychological Association, 2023).

A lack of inclusion, particularly for those from marginalized identities, can result in feelings of invisibility or alienation (Mor, Gündemir, & van der Toorn, 2025). And when calm and emotional regulation are not modeled or encouraged, being overwhelmed becomes a default state. Emotional dysregulation at the organizational level often mirrors the emotional state of those in leadership (Brackett,

2019). Adults may carry stress home with them, have trouble sleeping, or dread returning to work, all of which are early warning signs of burnout (Savill-Smith & Scanlan, 2022).

These emotions often reveal themselves in how educators show up at work. Some begin to pull away from their colleagues and quietly opt out of team efforts (Jennings, 2015). Others start to sound more discouraged and question the value of their contributions or express a growing sense of hopelessness. Resistance to new initiatives may not stem from laziness or obstinance but from a genuine fear of failure or humiliation (Brown, 2018). As the demands of the job wear down teachers, the sense of purpose that once fueled their work can begin to fade. Burnout can quietly take root, showing up through patterns like frequent absences or emotional detachment (Maslach & Leiter, 2016). When this happens across a staff, it starts to erode the overall tone of the building. That shift in adult climate doesn't stay contained; it's the emotional environment students step into every day (Kraft & Lyon, 2024).

When Students Don't Feel Emotionally Safe

Students, like the adults who support them, are profoundly shaped by their sense of emotional safety; however, for students, the impact can run even deeper. When trust isn't present, they may hold back from asking questions or sharing what they really think. Some become afraid of how others might react, unsure if they'll be taken seriously or treated with kindness. That kind of fear makes it difficult to engage fully, which limits both their learning and their ability to grow emotionally (Minahan & Rappaport, 2012).

A lack of belonging shows up as social withdrawal or, conversely, attention-seeking behavior. Students may isolate themselves or act out in attempts to reclaim connection (Cipriano et al., 2023). When students feel disrespected through tone, inequitable treatment, or microaggressions, they may shut down or lash out. These reactions are often misinterpreted as defiance rather than distress (Darling-Hammond & Cook-Harvey, 2018).

In unpredictable environments, students live with uncertainty. In other words, they may not know what their teacher expects or what consequences will be applied. This lack of clarity can breed anxiety, hypervigilance, and task avoidance (Osher & Berg, 2018).

A lack of inclusion, whether based on race, gender, ability, language, or identity, can lead students to suppress their authentic selves. In efforts to blend in, they may mimic their peers or hide parts of themselves (Terrell, Terrell, Lindsey, & Lindsey, 2018).

When emotional regulation is not taught or supported, dysregulation becomes the norm. Students may have meltdowns, refuse to comply, or display explosive behavior. None of these behaviors can be addressed effectively without tending to the root cause: a lack of emotional safety (Jones, McGarrah, & Kahn, 2019).

These emotional and behavioral patterns are not random; they are survival strategies. When students don't feel safe, their brains activate the amygdala, which is the fight, flight, or freeze response. This activation shuts down executive functions responsible for memory, focus, planning, and reflection (Holland, 2025). In these mental states, learning becomes nearly impossible. Without emotional safety, even the instructional strategies with the highest effect sizes fail to take root. It's not that students don't want to learn; their brains are too busy trying to survive.

Figure 2.2 is a summary of how the lack of each key sub-emotion of emotional safety could affect *behavior* for adults and students.

Missing Sub-Emotion or Trait	Adult Impact	Student Impact
Trust	Hypervigilance, guarded behavior, reluctance to collaborate	Fear of judgment, hesitancy to participate or ask for help
Belonging	Isolation, disengagement, or feeling undervalued; risk of burnout	Withdrawal, acting out, or chronic absenteeism
Respect	Demoralization, resentment, withdrawal from team dynamics	Low self-esteem or disruptive behavior
Predictability	Anxiety, confusion, reduced performance and confidence	Behavioral outbursts, disengagement from learning
Inclusion	Feeling invisible or unwelcome; self-censorship	Shame about identity, disengagement, mimicry to fit in
Calm	Emotional reactivity, poor focus, and conflict escalation	Inability to focus, emotional shutdown, or lashing out

Figure 2.2: Behavioral impact when people don't feel emotionally safe.

*Visit **go.SolutionTree.com/schoolimprovement** for a free reproducible version of this figure.*

When safety is missing, so are some of the most human ideals we long to feel at work and in school (American Psychological Association, 2024). You won't find curiosity in the same way. It's hard to ask a question when you're afraid of how it will land. You'll see less risk taking because why step forward when stepping back feels safer? Without safety, laughter becomes rare, feedback feels like criticism, and connection gives way to isolation. People don't lean into hard work when they feel like they're bracing for impact.

Maybe you've seen it in a student like Mason, a quiet sixth grader in a large urban middle school, who never gets in trouble but never raises his hand either. He learned that drawing attention to himself often ends badly, so he stays small, unnoticed, and safe. Or maybe it's Ms. Jones, a veteran teacher in a small mountain district, who used to be the first to try new things but has recently grown hesitant and withdrawn. A previous misstep was met with blame, not support, and now she sticks to what she knows. And then there's you as you wonder how to reach them, how to shift the air in the room, and how to create a place where people don't just show up but show up *open*.

Creating the Conditions for Emotional Safety (Adult to Adult)

A healthy school climate starts with the adults (Mutonyi, Slåtten, Lien, & González-Piñero, 2022). Before we can ask educators to create safe, supportive spaces for students, we must ask, *Do they feel safe themselves*? Not just physically safe, but emotionally safe. Safe to be human, speak honestly, take risks, admit mistakes, and ask for help without fear of judgment or punishment. Emotional safety is the soil where trust, collaboration, and innovation grow (Putra, Setiadi, Gautama, Bandur, & Sundjaja, 2025). Without it, everything else we try to plant, including new initiatives, instructional shifts, and culture-building efforts, will struggle to take root.

When educators feel emotionally safe, they are far more likely to extend those same conditions to students (Dreer-Goethe, 2025). Safety becomes the undercurrent of every conversation, every hallway interaction, and every team meeting. It shows up when someone lingers after a hard conversation to say, "Are we good?" Or when a teacher shares a lesson that flopped and hears, "Thanks for being honest. I've been there, too." These moments may seem small, but they're not. They are the architecture of trust.

Trust among adults changes everything.

- When the staff room is a place where people breathe easier instead of bracing themselves . . .
- When collaboration doesn't feel like compliance but connection . . .
- When feedback is framed with dignity instead of defensiveness . . .

That's when safety comes to life.

The following sections focus on practical ways to strengthen a sense of safety for the adults who work in our schools. We begin with strategies that can be implemented within individual school buildings—actions that leaders and staff members can take to help ensure educators feel safe in their daily work. We then widen the lens to look at the district level, highlighting strategies that district office leaders and employees across the system can use to reinforce and sustain that same sense of safety.

Safety Strategies for Adults Within a School

The following are some practical sample strategies that help cultivate a sense of safety among staff. These strategies are not an exhaustive list but rather a sampling of meaningful strategies you can try or use as examples to guide you in customizing strategies that meet your specific needs. Used with intention, these practices can begin to soften guarded spaces, rebuild fractured trust, and create the kind of workplace where people aren't just surviving but healing, growing, and thriving together. (You can find a list of the adult-to-adult emotional safety strategies in the appendix, page 147.)

Protect Planning Time and Boundaries

One of the most overlooked aspects of physical safety for educators is time. Specifically, time that is respected, protected, and free from unnecessary interruption. When teachers feel like every moment of their day is spoken for, including the time meant for planning, regrouping, or using the restroom, it sends a message that their needs don't matter. Protecting this time is more than a scheduling courtesy; it's a form of professional dignity. In one district, leadership created a non-interruption zone during teacher planning periods: no pop-ins, no last-minute asks, no surprise walkthroughs. Teachers reported feeling more grounded and less rushed, which led to more thoughtful instruction and lower stress levels (Phan et al., 2025). Physical safety means more than locked doors; it also means time to breathe.

Prioritize Safe and Functional Workspaces

A climate of safety includes the spaces we walk through and work in every day. Cracked tiles, broken chairs, inaccessible staff bathrooms, or poor lighting might seem like small issues, but they signal something bigger. When adults work in environments that are neglected or unsafe, it impacts morale and undermines a sense of worth (Slil, Iyiola, Alzubi, & Aljuhmani, 2025). On the flip side, when staff spaces are maintained, clean, and thoughtfully arranged, it communicates respect. At an urban high school in Atlanta, a principal conducted a staff space audit by asking teachers to note any physical improvements needed in their classrooms and common areas. Within a month, broken furniture was replaced, bathroom lighting was fixed, and the staff lounge was modernized to entice staff usage. The shift in mood was immediate. People began using the space, talking more, and staying later—not because they had to, but because it felt good to be there. Physical safety is also emotional safety; it's just expressed through space.

Begin With Emotional Check-Ins

One of the most human things we can do for one another is to simply ask, "How are you, really?" Check-ins help normalize emotional expression, build empathy, and create a sense of psychological safety (CASEL, 2020; Kahn, 1990). Starting meetings or team sessions with brief emotional check-ins can shift the entire tone of a group. It might be as simple as asking, "What's one word that describes how you're feeling today?" or using a sentence starter like "Today, I'm feeling ____________ because ____________." These small openings give permission for people to show up honestly, without needing to armor up. When adults feel safe enough to name their emotional state, even briefly, it normalizes vulnerability and builds connection.

At a small rural elementary school in eastern Colorado, the principal launched a weekly Wellness Wednesday, in which staff kicked off their morning with a three-word emotional check-in. Over time, staff reported not only stronger relationships but also more productive collaboration and higher trust scores on climate surveys. It turns out that when people feel seen, they show up differently (Wowor & Dewi, 2022).

Make Feedback Safe and Expected

Feedback should never feel like a trap. It should feel like care. Regular, structured feedback builds trust and reduces defensiveness (Stone & Heen, 2014). When giving and receiving feedback is a routine part of professional life, it loses its sting and gains power. A simple shift in language using sentence frames like "I noticed . . ." or "I wonder . . ." can turn evaluation into inquiry. Leaders can model this by offering feedback privately, anchoring it in shared goals, and asking reciprocal questions like, "Is there anything I can do to support you better?" This signals that feedback is a two-way street. In schools that use the Marzano High Reliability framework (Marzano, Warrick, & Acosta, 2024)—a research-validated school improvement framework that identifies five levels of effective school conditions—walkthroughs are framed with appreciative and inquiry-based language, which reduces tension and builds openness. Karin Hurt and David Dye (2025) explain that when feedback feels safe, it becomes a tool for growth, not a source of stress.

Implement Rituals to Create Predictability

Adults crave predictability just as much as students do (Xanthopoulou, Patitsa, Sotiropoulou, Chalaris, & Kalogiannidis, 2025). In fact, predictable routines are one of the most underused tools in building emotional safety. Predictability supports emotional regulation and decreases stress responses (Kadović, Mikšić, & Lovrić, 2023). When meetings begin and end on time, follow a consistent agenda, or open with familiar rituals, they become more than just gatherings; they become grounding moments. Predictability says: *You can trust this space.*

At a school in Minnesota, staff meetings always follow the same four-part structure: (1) celebrations, (2) data highlights, (3) problems of practice, and (4) commitments. That rhythm helps educators feel prepared, reduces anxiety, and fosters a sense of shared purpose. It's not flashy, but it's powerful. Predictability is one way we can show respect.

Use Shared Language to Navigate Conflict

Conflict is inevitable in any workplace, but harm doesn't have to be. When teams use a shared language to name emotions, express needs, and repair ruptures, conflict becomes a tool for growth instead of a trigger for division (Terrell et al., 2021). Without that shared vocabulary, misunderstandings grow heavier, silences grow longer, and collaboration erodes.

In one district, a disagreement arose between two team leads about how instructional minutes were being allocated. Instead of avoiding the issue, they used language from a norms agreement developed at the start of the year: "I want to check this with curiosity, not assumption." That phrase, which had been rooted in shared expectations, helped them move the conversation forward without blame. Common language doesn't prevent conflict; it helps us stay connected while we move through it. Safety lives in the words we choose.

Model Emotional Regulation

Calm is contagious. When leaders and team leads model emotional regulation, they create a climate where others feel safe enough to regulate, too (McAdoo, 2025). This doesn't mean leaders have to be stoic or emotionless; it means being intentional in how we respond. Saying aloud, "I need a breath before I respond," or "Let's take a quick pause before we move forward," models self-awareness and gives others permission to do the same. Emotional contagion is real, and regulated adults help co-regulate others (Brackett, 2019). One veteran principal shared how, after challenging meetings, she intentionally pauses and says, "I want to be thoughtful, not reactive." That small gesture has transformed the emotional tone of her team. When leaders stay grounded, the ripple effects can be felt in every corner of the building.

Safety Strategies for Adults in District-to-School Leadership

Safety at the school level is profoundly shaped by the clarity and consistency modeled at the district level. Principals cannot cultivate environments of psychological and physical safety for staff if they themselves are navigating conflicting directives, unclear expectations, or punitive supervisory relationships. District leaders set the emotional tone that cascades downward. Steadiness creates steadiness, and pressure creates pressure.

The following strategies help district leaders ensure every campus leader feels grounded enough to cultivate safety for their school communities.

Establish Predictable Communication Rhythms

Districts can dramatically reduce anxiety by creating a simple, consistent communication cadence for principals. Examples such as Monday updates, Thursday reminders, or standing weekly calls create predictable rhythms that decrease cognitive load and help principals plan ahead rather than brace for surprises. When leaders know what to expect, they can offer the same predictability to their staff.

Protect Principals From Initiative Overload

Safety deteriorates when leaders feel like they are being bombarded from above. District leadership can model emotional safety by auditing and streamlining expectations; eliminating redundant initiatives; and clarifying what is *required*, what is *recommended*, and what is *optional*. When principals experience reduced overwhelm, they become calmer, more present, and more able to create predictable environments for educators.

Respond to Crises With Support, Not Scrutiny

When something goes wrong on a campus, such as an incident, a complaint, or even a mistake, district leaders can build emotional safety by leading with curiosity rather than immediate criticism. Saying, "I'm here to support you; walk me through what happened," communicates partnership instead of fear. This approach strengthens trust and models the exact kind of emotional regulation we expect principals to exhibit with their teams.

Adult-to-Adult Safety Strategies Created With AI

These strategies, while simple on the surface, are powerful acts of care, consistency, and professionalism. We acknowledge that your specific context may require additional strategies or customizing the strategies we shared. Therefore, we created the following AI prompt that you can use as a guide to create or customize adult-to-adult safety strategies.

> Using the following sub-emotion(s)/trait(s)/strategy of emotional safety: [insert one or more definition(s) of a specific sub-emotion(s)/trait(s)/strategy from this section: trust, belonging, respect, predictability, inclusion, calm], help me design adult-to-adult safety strategies tailored to my specific context: [describe your school/department/team type, your staff culture, challenges, goals]. Please propose three to five simple and doable strategy options that fit my needs.

The following is a sample prompt and the AI-generated response. As all teams and educators should do when working with generative AI responses, we have reviewed and edited the following output for additional clarity and accuracy.

> **PROMPT:** Using the following sub-emotion(s)/trait(s)/strategy of emotional safety: trust, belonging, and respect, help me design adult-to-adult safety strategies tailored to my specific context: I am an instructional coach in a comprehensive urban high school who works with all teachers. Please propose three to five simple and doable strategy options that fit my needs.

RESPONSE: The following are **three to five simple, doable, high-impact adult-to-adult emotional safety strategies** designed *specifically* for your role as an instructional coach in a comprehensive urban high school. Each strategy focuses on **trust, belonging, and respect**—the three sub-emotions that most strongly anchor adult safety in schools.

Adult-to-Adult Emotional Safety Strategies for an Instructional Coach

Focused on Trust + Belonging + Respect

1. **"Confidential Coaching Agreements" to Build Trust**

   Purpose: Establish psychological safety by making confidentiality explicit and consistent.

   What to Do:

   - At the start of every coaching cycle, create a short, one-page "Coaching Agreement" outlining expectations—especially confidentiality.
   - Include language such as: *"Coaching conversations stay between us unless you explicitly ask me to share something."*
   - Review it together and invite teachers to add anything that would help them feel safer.

   Why It works: Clear boundaries reduce fear of judgment or evaluation. Teachers begin to trust that coaching is a partnership, not surveillance.

   Success indicator: Teachers begin sharing vulnerabilities, questions, or worries they previously kept private.

2. **"Belonging Rounds" During Department or School Visits With Collaborative Teams**

   Purpose: Help teachers feel seen, connected, and part of a community—not isolated in their classrooms.

   What to Do:

   - When visiting collaborative teams or department meetings, start with a two-minute check-in prompt such as the following.
     * *"Name one small win from your week."*

    * *"Name one thing a colleague did that helped you."*
  - Keep it quick, warm, and optional, but model participation.

Why it works: These tiny rituals normalize connection, reduce isolation, and create micro-moments of belonging without adding the burden of another meeting.

Success indicator: The room softens—people smile, speak more freely, and reference each other's wins later in the meeting.

3. **"Respect-First Feedback Framework" in Coaching Conversations**

Purpose: Ensure teachers experience feedback as respectful, humanizing, and affirming—not evaluative or corrective.

What to Do:

Use a three-step feedback process every time you debrief an observation.

1. Start with contribution: "Here's something you did today that mattered . . ."
2. Honor the teacher's voice: "What felt most successful to you?"
3. Offer a single, respectful stretch: "What's one small next step you want to try?"

Why it works: When teachers feel respected as professionals—and treated as partners—they are more willing to take risks and reflect deeply.

Success indicator: Teachers leave conversations energized rather than depleted.

4. **"Opt-In Peer Observation Walks" to Build Belonging and Trust**

Purpose: Reduce isolation and build collegial safety by creating a voluntary, low-stakes way for teachers to learn from one another.

What to Do:

- Organize short, informal peer walks (ten to fifteen minutes).
- Teachers sign up voluntarily.

- Handle the logistics (coverage, schedule, focus).
- Afterward, facilitate a five-minute reflection.
    - * *"What's something you appreciated?"*
    - * *"What might you try?"*

Why it works: Seeing colleagues teach builds community and respect. Voluntary participation protects psychological safety.

Success indicator: Teachers begin requesting to visit each other's classrooms without prompting.

5. **"Respect and Recognition Notes" From Coach to Teacher**

Purpose: Reinforce emotional safety by showing respect for teachers' effort, growth, and humanity.

What to Do:

- Keep a stack of small cards or sticky notes.
- After walkthroughs, planning meetings, or tough weeks, leave specific, sincere notes such as the following.
    - * *"I noticed how patiently you worked with that new student today."*
    - * *"Your modeling of conflict resolution was powerful."*
- Focus on *efforts witnessed*, not results.

Why it works: Small recognitions build trust and reinforce a culture where respect and humanity come first.

Success indicator: Teachers begin keeping your notes—pinned to desks, taped inside planners, or saved on bulletin boards. (OpenAI, 2025b)

Creating the Conditions for Emotional Safety (Adult to Student)

So now, we turn our attention to our students, who need the same care, the same clarity, the same consistency we've just offered to one another. They are watching, listening, and absorbing the emotional tone of our buildings and our classrooms. And they are asking, without ever saying it out loud, *Am I safe here?*

Let's talk about what it looks like to answer that question with action.

Students' emotional safety is the foundation on which everything else grows (Han, Liu, & Lv, 2022). Before students can engage deeply, take academic risks, or build meaningful relationships, they need to know, *truly know*, they are safe in our presence. Not only safe from harm but also safe from shame. Safe to ask the so-called wrong questions. Safe to try and fail. Safe to be seen.

Safety in the classroom isn't about softening expectations; it's about strengthening relationships. It's about being the kind of adult who can hold both accountability and compassion in the same breath.

A Safety Story

In a tribal K–8 school on Navajo Nation land, every morning begins with a short community gathering in which students and teachers greet one another in Diné Bizaad. For a fourth grader named Kai, these few minutes change everything. He often arrived withdrawn, shoulders tight, carrying worries from home. But when his teacher called his name in Navajo and invited him to join the circle, he stepped forward with a small smile. "It reminds him who he is," she said. Throughout the year, Kai began participating more and connecting with classmates he previously avoided. In spaces where cultural identity is honored, safety becomes more than a feeling; it becomes a strengthening of self.

When students feel emotionally safe, they don't just behave better; they learn better (Clausen et al., 2025). They begin to trust that school isn't a place where they must perform or protect themselves, but a place where they can learn and grow—not only academically, but also socially and emotionally.

It's important to remember that safety isn't a one-time event. Instead, it's built moment by moment in how we greet students at the door, respond to their mistakes, and recover when we get it wrong. It's built into what we say, or don't, when they're hurting. It's in the tone we use when correcting behavior, the patience we offer when they're not ready to learn, and the way we look them in the eye after a hard day and say, "I'm glad you're here." Students' emotional and physical safety is the foundation on which everything else is built. Before they can engage deeply, take academic risks, or build meaningful relationships, they need to know, truly know, that they are safe in our presence.

You might already be doing this work every day, even if no one calls it out. Maybe you're the teacher who keeps snacks for students who never eat breakfast, the counselor who writes notes of encouragement just because, or the paraprofessional who always remembers which student needs the seat by the door. These small gestures tell students: *You matter here. You are safe here.*

Safety Strategies for Students

The following sample strategies, while not exhaustive, are intended to help you support physical and emotional safety across all classrooms and content areas. (You can find a list of the adult-to-student emotional safety strategies in the appendix, page 147.)

Ensure Clear, Consistent Safety Procedures

For students to feel physically safe, they need to know what to expect in the event of uncertainty or danger. According to the Connecticut General Assembly House Bill 7009 (2025), safety procedures shouldn't be scary or performative; they should be practical, age-appropriate, and clear. When students know where to go, who to trust, and what to do during drills or emergencies, schools reduce fear and build confidence (Ibrahim, Kiran, Usman Dar, & Mahnaz, 2025). At a middle school in Michigan, leaders revised their safety drills to include follow-up circles, where students could talk about what felt confusing or scary. Teachers noticed that students were more attentive in future drills and expressed greater trust in the adults around them. Physical safety doesn't begin and end with locked doors. It's also about clarity, communication, and care.

Design Safe, Welcoming Spaces

The way a room feels says something before a word is ever spoken. Harsh lighting, cluttered walkways, or impersonal decorations can make students feel on edge, especially those with sensory sensitivities or histories of trauma (Hanley et al., 2017). On the other hand, soft seating, clear pathways, calming colors, and personalized touches can send the message that students are safe. A fifth-grade teacher in Arizona redesigned her classroom with sensory-friendly corners and student artwork on the walls. One student said, "It feels like a room that wants me to be in it." Physical environments are not neutral; they either help students regulate or push them into survival mode.

Greet Students by Name

Greeting students at the door increases engagement and reduces disruptive behavior (Cook, Lyon, Kubergovic, Browning Wright, & Zhang, 2015). It seems simple, but greeting a student by name is one of the most powerful signals of emotional safety we can send. A consistent, warm greeting at the door tells students: *You're expected here, you're known, and you matter*. It's a moment to set the tone and reestablish connection. A K–8 teacher in rural Nevada created a greeting menu with icons that let students choose how they wanted to be welcomed: a fist bump, wave, or compliment. Students loved the autonomy and ritual. Greeting students by name is more than manners; it is belonging in action.

Build Predictable Routines

Predictability is one of the most underrated forms of safety we can offer. Predictable structures improve academic outcomes and student self-regulation (Minahan & Rappaport, 2012). For students, especially those who live with trauma, anxiety, or frequent change, predictable routines are like handrails. They help students focus less on what's coming next and more on what they're learning in the moment. An eleventh-grade English teacher starts every morning with the same written message on the board: "Here's what you can expect today." Students say it helps them feel prepared, calm, and engaged. Predictable routines reduce uncertainty and make space for learning to happen.

Use Calm Corners and Regulation Tools

Sometimes, safety doesn't mean pushing through; it means stepping away. Offering students a space to self-regulate before they escalate is an act of respect and care. Self-regulation spaces lower cortisol levels and prevent escalation (Khng, 2023). Calm corners aren't time-outs; instead, they are time-ins or opportunities for students to reset with dignity. In a New Jersey urban elementary school, every classroom includes a Take Five zone with soft seating, fidget toys, and calming prompts. Teachers report fewer meltdowns and quicker recoveries. When students are taught how to use these spaces, they become part of a healthy coping tool kit, not a place of punishment.

Teach Language for Emotional Repair

Students often lack the words to say what they really mean, especially in moments of frustration or shame. Teaching and modeling language for emotional repair gives students the tools to return to safety when they've crossed a line (Sullins, Turner,

Kim, & Barber, 2024). When a student lashes out, verbally attacks, curses, or disrupts, it's often not about defiance but instead about being overwhelmed, unskilled, or unseen.

In a middle school classroom, a student screamed profanity at a teacher after being redirected. The teacher, instead of escalating, calmly said, "You're allowed to be upset, but you're not allowed to be unsafe. I'm here when you're ready to talk." Later, they sat down and used a simple reflection tool with prompts like, *What happened? What were you feeling? What do you need next time?* Over time, those tools became part of the classroom culture. Students began using phrases like, "I lost control, but I'm trying again," and "Can I reset?" Emotional safety grows when we not only expect better behavior but also teach the language to get there.

Create Opportunities for Student Voice

Students feel safe when they feel heard. Student voice isn't just about big decisions; it's about everyday interactions in which students get to express how they're feeling, what they need, or how they learn best. Student voice improves motivation, engagement, and school climate (Quaglia & Corso, 2014). One high school teacher in an Oregon urban middle school uses a weekly Pulse Check form with questions like, "What's one thing you wish I knew?" One student wrote, "This is the first time I felt like my opinion mattered." Giving students voice helps them feel like full participants in their own education and reinforces that their experiences are valid.

Protect Identity and Promote Inclusion

Students do not feel safe if they feel erased. Classrooms that affirm students' identities, such as their cultural and linguistic backgrounds, gender identities, and neurodiversity, signal to every student: *You are welcome here exactly as you are.* This means using inclusive language, offering diverse representation in the curriculum, and responding swiftly to moments of harm. Identity-affirming classrooms reduce anxiety and increase academic success for marginalized students (Hsueh et al., 2021). A teacher once noticed students mocking a peer's accent. She paused the class, named what happened, and led a restorative conversation about respect. That one moment reshaped how her students treated one another moving forward. Inclusion is not a poster on the wall; it's a daily commitment to creating safety through dignity.

Adult-to-Student Emotional Safety Strategies Created With AI

The strategies we outlined are grounded in one core belief: Every student deserves to feel safe enough to learn, speak, make mistakes, and be fully themselves. We recognize that your unique context may call for further adaptation or refinement of these strategies, or you may be seeking more. To support this process, we developed the following AI prompt, which is designed to help you generate or tailor adult-to-student safety strategies to meet your specific needs.

> Using the following sub-emotion(s)/trait(s)/strategy of emotional safety: [insert one or more definition(s) of a specific sub-emotion(s)/trait(s)/strategy from this section: trust, belonging, respect, predictability, inclusion, calm], help me design adult-to-student safety strategies tailored to my specific context: [describe your school/department/team type, your staff culture, challenges, goals]. Please propose three to five simple and doable strategy options that fit my needs.

The following is a sample prompt and the AI-generated response. As all teams and educators should do when working with generative AI responses, we have reviewed and edited the following output for additional clarity and accuracy.

> **PROMPT:** Using the following sub-emotion(s)/trait(s)/strategy of emotional safety: inclusion and calm, help me design adult-to-student safety strategies tailored to my specific context: I am a kindergarten teacher. Please propose three to five simple and doable strategy options that fit my needs.
>
> **RESPONSE:** Below are **five simple, developmentally appropriate, high-impact safety strategies** designed *specifically* for your context as a **kindergarten teacher**, using the core emotional safety traits of **inclusion** and **calm**. Each strategy helps young learners feel welcomed, grounded, and secure—two conditions essential for learning in early childhood.
>
> **Adult-to-Student Emotional Safety Strategies for a Kindergarten Classroom**
>
> ***Focused on Inclusion + Calm***
>
> 1. **"Morning Belonging Circle" (two to three minutes daily)**

Purpose: Make every student feel included the moment they walk in.

What to Do:

- Students sit in a quick circle.
- Greet each child by name with eye contact.
    * *"Good morning, Maya. I'm glad you're here."*
- Students repeat a simple belonging affirmation like, *"We are all welcome in this room."*

Why it works: Consistent rituals anchor students in belonging and calm from the very start of the day.

Success indicator: Students enter more regulated, with fewer early-morning tears, arguments, or clinginess.

2. **"Calming Choice Spots" for Emotional Regulation**

Purpose: Give students agency for managing their emotions in a safe, nonpunitive way.

What to Do:

- Set up two small areas.
    * **The Cozy Corner** (pillows, books, soft textures)
    * **The Breathing Spot** (breathing visuals, glitter jar, calm cards)
- Students may choose either spot when overwhelmed.
- Teach that these are "tools to feel safe," not consequences.

Why it works: Choice promotes inclusion (every student can choose what works for them), and predictable calm spaces prevent escalation.

Success indicator: Students begin independently using tools instead of melting down.

3. **"Inclusion Jobs" So Every Student Contributes**

Purpose: Build safety through predictable roles and community responsibility.

What to Do:

- Create simple rotating jobs: greeter, line leader, kindness helper, materials friend, plant helper, and so on.

- Every student has a turn *before anyone repeats*.
- Emphasize that the classroom needs everyone to work.

Why it works: Inclusion strengthens safety—students feel secure when they know they belong and have a meaningful part in the community.

Success indicator: Students remind each other of their roles and show pride when it's "their day."

4. **"Calm-First Transitions"**

   Purpose: Reduce chaos during the most dysregulating parts of the day.

   What to Do:

   - Before transitions, pause for a ten-to-fifteen-second calm cue.
     * Soft chime
     * Deep breath together
     * "Hands on heart, hands on belly"
     * Short stretch
   - Then, state a simple expectation: *"When we feel calm, we can walk safely to the carpet."*

   Why it works: Predictable, calming rituals cue the nervous system to settle, increasing students' emotional safety and reducing conflict.

   Success indicator: Transitions become smoother, quieter, and faster.

5. **"Friendship Welcome Rituals" for Inclusive Peer Connections**

   Purpose: Strengthen emotional safety by building inclusive peer relationships.

   What to Do:

   - Teach two or three simple, safe greeting options students can offer each other every morning.
     * Wave
     * High-five
     * Heart hands

- Students choose how they want to greet peers—no touching required.
- Rotate partners so everyone feels included.

Why it works: Small, structured social rituals help prevent exclusion patterns and create a calm, loving atmosphere.

Success indicator: Students begin greeting one another without prompting and show fewer conflicts during free play. (OpenAI, 2025b)

When we greet students by name, create predictable routines, offer calm spaces, protect their identities, teach language for emotional repair, and listen with care, we aren't just managing behavior or supporting learning; we are shaping the climate they live in every day. That climate becomes the lens through which they see school, themselves, and their own potential.

Safety is not something we wait for students to create. It is something educators establish first through the environments and interactions we shape. It underpins how we arrange our classrooms, how we respond when students are dysregulated, how we repair when we misstep, how we teach students to restore when they make a mistake, and how we create space for them to be heard without fear. Physical safety tells students they are protected and cared for; emotional safety tells them they are respected and they belong. Both are essential. When students trust that school is a place where they are safe to move, speak, rest, ask, and try without harm or shame, they engage more fully and show up more freely. Adult-to-student safety isn't extra—it's foundational. And it is one of the most powerful forces for building a school climate where students don't just show up but thrive.

Physical safety tells students they are protected and cared for; emotional safety tells them they are respected and they belong.

Issues That Transcend School Climate

If you have repeatedly come to this chapter seeking help to feel safe, you may discover that the problems you are facing are bigger than climate. Repeated climate patterns are a symptom of the culture. The school's culture manifests in how people behave based on what they believe, including yourself. The strategies in this chapter are intended to help adults and students *feel safe* in the moment.

If you have determined that your issue goes beyond immediate climate strategies, we offer you insights in the following sections. The first section focuses on self-care or educator wellness because we know the well-being of adults significantly impacts the day-to-day climate. The second section addresses school culture because if those in your care feel unsafe because of actions or inactions on the part of others in your school or district, then culture will be impacted.

Emotional Safety and Self-Care or Educator Wellness

Everything in this chapter points to a powerful truth: Self-care or educator wellness cannot exist without safety. When adults move through their days bracing for criticism, absorbing the stress of unpredictability, or working in environments that feel unfair, the nervous system shifts into survival mode (Van der Kolk, 2014). Survival mode is incompatible with sustained well-being. You cannot practice meaningful self-care in an ecosystem that constantly signals threat. Chronic stress in unsafe climates doesn't just stay at school; it follows educators home in the form of exhaustion, sleep disruption, and health concerns (American Psychological Association, 2023; Maslach & Leiter, 2016).

At the same time, emotional safety is something we create *for ourselves* and *with* one another.

To create your own sense of safety, you may experiment with any of the following strategies (Boogren, 2018).

- Record your worries in writing to get them out of your constant thoughts.
- Reach out and talk to someone you trust about your worries and stressors.
- Stick to a schedule if consistency makes you feel safe.
- Listen to calming music, inhale a calming scent, or engage in calming activities such as mindful breathing, meditation, yoga, or Tai Chi.
- Talk to a financial adviser to ensure you're saving and investing wisely.
- Memorize essential phone numbers.

Because emotions are contagious, the benefits of educator self-care and emotional safety don't stop with adults. Research on emotional contagion shows that students and staff take their cues from the adults who set the tone (Brackett, 2019; Hatfield, Cacioppo, & Rapson, 1994). Regulated, grounded educators model calm, curiosity, and repair, and they create the very conditions students need to feel safe, take risks, and learn deeply. Without safety, self-care becomes reactionary—an attempt to refill what keeps being drained. With safety, however, self-care becomes proactive—a steady foundation that supports all stakeholders. When we build emotionally safe schools, we are building the conditions where adults can flourish, and flourishing adults create flourishing students (American Psychological Association, 2023).

Emotional Safety and School Culture

When safety is consistently lacking, despite sincere efforts to apply climate strategies, the root cause is often embedded in the culture. In these cases, it's not about what's happening in the moment, but what's been happening over time. Culture reflects the deeply held beliefs, norms, and values that guide behavior across a school or district (Acosta, 2026). If patterns of fear, silence, or blame persist, they are not climate flukes; they are cultural signatures.

An ineffective culture cannot be rebranded with good intentions or occasional kindness. It must be rebuilt through deep, consistent, and collective change. If your workplace punishes vulnerability, ignores harm, or protects harmful behavior under the guise of tradition or hierarchy, you are not facing a climate issue; you are staring directly at the culture.

This kind of reflection takes courage. It means asking hard questions, such as the following.

- What behaviors are rewarded here?
- What is considered "normal" even when it causes harm?
- Whose voices are heard, and whose are dismissed?

These aren't surface questions; they cut to the root. And the answers help determine whether your school's culture is built on fear or on trust.

Changing culture requires more than programs or slogans. It requires aligned action from both leadership and those courageous enough to disrupt unhealthy norms. It means moving from compliance to integrity. From silence to truth-telling. It means refusing to participate in practices that harm even when it's easier to go along.

If you are in a system where unsafe behaviors are normalized or ignored, your feelings of discomfort are not a failure; they're a form of wisdom. That discomfort is your internal climate warning you that something in the culture needs repair. Acosta (2026) notes that if you recognize a pattern of unsafe behavior in your school's culture, you don't need to wait for a systemwide overhaul to begin meaningful change. You can start where you are.

As an educator, your greatest influence lies in the subculture you help shape: your grade-level team, your hallway, your classroom, and the colleagues with whom you eat lunch. You can disrupt unsafe norms by modeling vulnerability, offering support, and refusing to normalize behavior that causes harm. Small actions, such as naming a concern, showing up with consistency, or setting a new tone, can all ripple outward.

For administrators, the work is broader but no less personal. Culture doesn't shift through mandates alone; it shifts when enough individual educators and subcultures begin living out new patterns of safe behaviors. Leaders must engage with subcultures directly—listen deeply, address misaligned and unsafe behaviors directly but with care, and build trust through aligned action. When done with intention, this kind of cultural work not only creates safer environments but also strengthens the whole system from the inside out.

The Climate We Create

Emotional safety is the steady, daily, fiercely intentional work that makes every other part of schooling possible. When adults and students alike know they can take risks, make mistakes, ask for help, and be fully themselves without fear of harm or humiliation, the entire climate shifts for the better. As you move forward, remember this: Safety isn't built in grand gestures but in a thousand small moments—your tone, your routines, your presence, your repairs, your boundaries, and the care you create for the adults and students you serve. These moments become the answer to the question every adult and student is silently asking: *Am I safe here?* When the answer is *yes*, flourishing becomes not just possible but inevitable.

Emotional safety is the steady, daily, fiercely intentional work that makes every other part of schooling possible.

CHAPTER 3

Feeling Supported

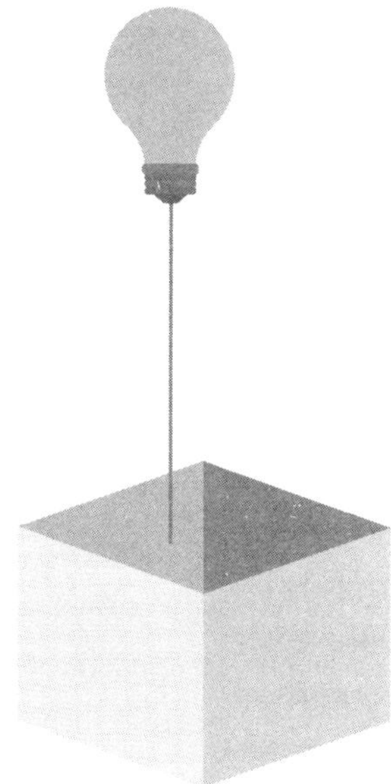

When I don't feel supported, it feels like everyone else knows what to do except me.

—SPECIAL EDUCATION STUDENT

When I don't feel supported, even small challenges start to feel impossible.

—MIDDLE SCHOOL ART TEACHER

When support is missing, leadership becomes lonely work and heavy in ways people rarely see.

—SUPERINTENDENT

You're here because you want the people around you to know they're not in it alone. You want students to believe that help will come when they ask for it—even when they're not quite sure how to ask. You want colleagues to know that when the work feels heavy, someone will notice and step in. You want your school to feel less like a collection of individuals and more like a team—a group of people who look out for one another and share the responsibility of supporting the students they serve.

That's what support really is: The quiet but powerful promise that no one has to carry the work entirely by themselves. In schools, where the demands are constant and the stakes feel high, that promise matters more than we sometimes realize. And the good news is that, just like the feeling of safety, support isn't mysterious or out of reach. It doesn't require elaborate systems or grand gestures. Support grows through small, consistent actions—one check-in, one thoughtful response, one moment of stepping alongside someone else.

Support often shows up in moments that are easy to overlook in the rush of the school day but are almost impossible to forget afterward. A mentor who sends a quick message to a teacher after a difficult conversation with a parent. A teammate who notices when someone is overwhelmed and quietly offers to take one thing off their plate. A leader who pauses long enough to listen fully before offering advice. A colleague who simply says, “I’ve got you,” and means it. These small gestures communicate something deeply human: *You matter here.*

Over time, these moments begin to accumulate. They shape the tone of a hallway conversation, the feeling inside a team meeting, and the willingness of people to speak honestly about challenges. In a supportive culture, asking for help feels normal rather than risky. People don’t have to pretend they have everything figured out. Instead, they know they are part of a community that will step forward when someone needs it.

When people feel supported, something important shifts. Educators are more willing to try new strategies, take instructional risks, and persist through difficult moments with students. They extend greater patience to one another. They remain connected to the deeper purpose that brought them into education in the first place. Support doesn’t remove the hard parts of the work, but it makes the work feel possible to carry together.

In this chapter, we examine practical, research-informed strategies for strengthening support in two essential areas: among adults and between adults and students. These strategies are intentionally simple and sustainable, grounded in everyday interactions that gradually build a stronger sense of support across a school community. Whether you serve at the district level, teach in a classroom, lead a campus, or contribute in a role that often happens behind the scenes, this chapter invites you into the meaningful work of creating supportive environments—because people are far more likely to grow, take risks, and improve when they know the support around them is real.

You Might Need This Chapter If . . .

You might need this chapter if your teachers say *yes* to requests but silently feel like they’re drowning; if hallway conversations have turned into venting sessions; if your strongest students suddenly stop submitting assignments; or if your colleagues stop sharing ideas during team meetings. These are all signs that indicate a need for increased support. You might also notice changes in tone. For example, you might see it in a teacher who used to advocate for innovative approaches to support students but now avoids participation at staff meetings. You might see it in a student who once sought help but now shrugs and says, "I don't care," instead of raising their hand and asking their teacher for clarification. These aren't just behavior shifts; they're evidence of the deeper truth that members of your school community no longer feel supported.

Support doesn't just change how we feel; it changes what we believe is possible. In schools, where stress can run high and resources can be stretched thin, the difference between engaging or detaching often comes down to whether someone feels supported. This chapter is an invitation to examine what support really looks like. It is not just a kind word but an actual pattern of care, fueled by both consistency and action. Together, we'll explore what it means to feel truly supported, not just by people, but also by systems and structures. In this chapter, we will share strategies that help us name and strengthen the support we give and receive. We offer practical ways to build a climate where no one must wonder if they matter or feel they must go it alone.

Support isn't just about getting help; it's about believing help is truly accessible. When support is thin, people begin carrying more than they can bear, and disconnection quietly spreads.

To perform a quick diagnostic check, use these questions to determine whether support is the feeling your climate needs most right now. (You can find the "Climate Chapter Diagnostic Tool" in the appendix, page 146.)

- Are your most capable people masking exhaustion while quietly drowning beneath the surface?
- Do students or colleagues stop asking for help because they assume no one has time to respond?
- Is access to resources, clarity, or guidance inconsistent enough to cause frustration or overwhelm?
- Has advocacy or mentorship become something that happens for a few rather than for all?
- Is isolation manifesting because support is unreliable?

If you can answer *yes* to most of these questions, this is a good place to start. If you have read this chapter before and understand the emotions and traits associated with the need to feel supported, you may choose to proceed straight to the strategy sections.

When People Don't Feel Supported

Support is a stabilizing force, and when it is absent, people start to disengage. Without encouragement, students may grow quiet or combative. Without advocacy, adults may retreat or resist. The absence of support often gets mistaken for defiance or disinterest, when it's really something much simpler: a loss of attachment (Bosmans, Bakermans-Kranenburg, Vervliet, Verhees, & van IJzendoorn, 2020).

Figure 3.1 provides a summary of the common emotional responses that emerge when key support-related sub-emotions are missing. (You can find a list of all the sub-emotions related to the four core feelings in the appendix, page 153.)

Missing Sub-Emotion or Trait	Common Emotions Experienced	Why These Emotions Arise
Encouragement	Self-doubt, shame, discouragement, isolation	Lack of belief from others leads to internalized doubt (Li & Singh, 2023).
Accessibility	Frustration, overwhelm, helplessness, burnout	Inaccessible resources lead to stress and underperformance (Bakker & Demerouti, 2017).
Responsiveness	Disconnection, mistrust, loneliness, resentment	Unmet needs cause feelings of abandonment or being unheard (Ray & Pana-Cryan, 2021).
Mentorship	Aimlessness, confusion, anxiety, lack of belonging	Absence of guidance leaves individuals directionless (Ocobock, Niclou, Loewen, Arslanian, Gibson, & Valeggia, 2022).
Advocacy	Injustice, fear, silence, vulnerability	Without champions, individuals feel exposed or unsafe (Peist, McMahon, Davis-Wright, & Keys, 2024).

Figure 3.1: Emotional impact when people don't feel supported.

Visit ***go.SolutionTree.com/schoolimprovement*** *for a free reproducible version of this figure.*

When Adults Don't Feel Supported

A lack of support doesn't stay hidden; it leaks into how adults relate to the people around them. A lack of encouragement can erode confidence, making educators second-guess their value. Without accessibility to resources or time, even the most committed staff can burn out trying to do more with less (Einav, Confino, Geva, & Margalit, 2024). When leaders or colleagues fail to respond, or when feedback disappears into a void, frustration builds and trust frays (Banwo, Khalifa, & Seashore Louis, 2022).

And then there's the quieter toll. Educators without mentors may feel stalled, unsure how to grow or who to turn to for guidance (Logis, Ren, Hudgens, & Barnett, 2025). When advocacy is missing, they may stop voicing needs altogether, thinking, "Why speak up if nothing changes?" The result is often disengagement masked as compliance. In other words, people still show up, but they're not fully engaged.

When Students Don't Feel Supported

Students notice when support disappears. A lack of encouragement makes students hesitate to try again after mistakes (Laslocky, 2021). They may stop asking questions because they assume no one believes they can improve. If they can't access help because help is hard to get, or the expectations are unclear, many give up—not because they don't care, but because they don't believe help is coming.

When students do not feel supported, or when their needs go unheard or unacknowledged, they may lash out or shut down (U.S. Department of Education, 2021). Without mentorship, students may detach, especially in adolescence, when guidance is critical (Stutey et al., 2022). When advocacy is missing, when no adult stands up for them in a moment of unfairness or invisibility, students internalize the message that they are on their own (Yeager, Dahl, & Dweck, 2017). That belief doesn't just affect behavior; it affects performance and, ultimately, student achievement. Figure 3.2 (page 70) outlines how the absence of each key sub-emotion may influence the behaviors of both adults and students.

When support is missing, people stop reaching. They retreat instead of risk. You'll see fewer questions, fewer collaborations, and fewer moments of creative energy. You might hear phrases like "What's the point?" or "I'll just figure it out." Sometimes, you won't hear anything at all because support isn't always withdrawn loudly; sometimes, it just fades until people learn not to expect it.

Missing Sub-Emotion or Trait	Adult Impact	Student Impact
Encouragement	Withdrawal, avoidance of challenge, impostor syndrome	Low participation, disengagement, fear of failure
Accessibility	Complaints, reduced productivity, avoidance	Dependency, frustration, task refusal
Responsiveness	Cynicism, disengagement, mistrust in leadership	Attention-seeking or shutdown behavior
Mentorship	Professional stagnation, lack of initiative	Repeated mistakes, academic drift
Advocacy	Defensiveness, silence in meetings, resistance	Behavior outbursts, feelings of invisibility

Figure 3.2: Behavioral impact when people don't feel supported.
*Visit **go.SolutionTree.com/schoolimprovement** for a free reproducible version of this figure.*

You might see it in a student like Leila, a ninth grader who's always polite but has stopped turning in work. She shrugs off reminders with, "It's fine. I'll catch up," but she never does. She's not lazy, she's lost. Or maybe it's Mr. Rivera, a talented assistant principal who now spends more time reacting to crises than mentoring staff. He used to share new ideas in leadership meetings, but now he just listens silently. He doesn't feel like he has the backing he once did. Or maybe it's you, wondering how to make sure people feel seen, well-resourced, and supported again.

Creating the Conditions for Support (Adult to Adult)

What many educators crave are not grand gestures, but consistent signals that reinforce: *You're not alone in this.*

Support among adults in a school community can feel like a lifeline. Educators spend their days pouring themselves into others by offering encouragement, problem solving in real time, regulating emotions, and responding to the needs of students and colleagues moment by moment. This steady outflow of care and attention is meaningful work, but it also requires intentional opportunities to refill our own cups. Without reciprocal systems of care, even the most passionate professionals can begin to fray. You might notice support fading when hallway conversations grow quieter, and staff engagement starts to deteriorate. In reality, what many educators crave are not grand gestures, but consistent signals that reinforce: *You're not alone in this.*

The following sections focus on practical ways to strengthen a sense of support for the adults who work in our schools. We begin with strategies that can be implemented within individual school buildings—actions that leaders and staff members can take to help ensure educators feel supported in their daily work. We then widen the lens to look at the district level, highlighting strategies that district office leaders and employees across the system can use to reinforce and sustain that same sense of support.

Support Strategies for Adults Within a School

The sample strategies that follow, while not intended to be a comprehensive set, are designed to reignite connection among the adults who make schools work. Again, these aren't time-intensive initiatives or new programs to add to already packed plates; instead, they are intentional ways to foster support across staff relationships. These strategies are designed to help restore the belief that someone will notice when we struggle and will celebrate not only what we do but also who we are. That's what helps adults stay, and thrive, in this work. (You can find a list of the adult-to-adult support strategies in the appendix, page 147.)

Hold Weekly Pulse Check Meetings

These are brief, ten-to-fifteen-minute structured team check-ins focused not on logistics but on how staff are *really* doing or feeling. During this time, each team member names one current stressor and one small win. This regular routine helps to normalize emotions and reduces isolation. Psychological safety, the belief that it's safe to ask for help or admit struggles, is a key driver of team effectiveness (Shahid & Din, 2021). Pulse checks can be done daily or, at the very least, once per week.

A Support Story

Every Monday, the seventh-grade team at a middle school starts their meeting with a quick stressor-and-win round. In less than ten minutes, teachers name one thing weighing on them and one thing going well. Last week, someone shared feeling overwhelmed by a behavior spike, and another celebrated a breakthrough with a quiet student. The simple routine helped everyone exhale, realize they weren't carrying things alone, and step into the week feeling more connected and supported.

Offer Visible Advocacy Among Educators

Support becomes more tangible when educators actively advocate for one another, not only behind closed doors but also in visible, public ways. This could look like a colleague speaking up in a staff meeting to affirm someone's idea or a paraprofessional ensuring that someone follows through on a concern raised by the custodian. This type of advocacy promotes the feeling of, *I've got your back*, especially when the stakes are high. When educators see and feel this kind of solidarity, they're more likely to take healthy risks and remain engaged in their work. In fact, research shows that support from colleagues, not just administrators, is a critical buffer against burnout and promotes stronger collaboration as well as retention (National Alliance for Public Charter Schools, 2023).

Encourage Formal and Informal Mentoring

Creating formal and informal spaces for mentorship, for both new educators as well as a form of emotional support for all staff, can help combat professional loneliness and isolation. Mentorship doesn't always have to be formal or hierarchical; even simple check-ins over coffee or shared planning time can provide an anchor for staff navigating various challenges. Formal and informal mentoring also creates space for shared celebration and reflection. Research shows that in a caring community, where teachers engage together in reflective dialogue and skill-sharing, mentoring not only supports teacher growth but also boosts retention and a sense of professional community (Weller Swanson & Caskey, 2024).

A Mentorship Story

At one high school, two teachers who share a hallway started meeting for a quick coffee each Friday morning. This was a simple ritual that soon became an informal mentorship. They swapped stories from the week, compared strategies, and celebrated small wins. What started as casual check-ins quickly became an anchor for both educators and eased the sense of isolation, which helped them feel more connected and supported. Over time, others joined in, turning a simple coffee chat into a small but powerful professional community.

Promote Openness Among Educators

Support must be visible. When educators across all roles make themselves accessible to one another, they send a powerful message: *We're in this together*. This might look like a teacher telling a colleague, "Come by during lunch if you want to talk through that lesson," or a staff member replying to a peer's concern with, "I'm around after dismissal. Let's figure it out together." When educators know who they can turn to, and when, they're less likely to feel isolated or stuck. When educators maintain open doors both literally and figuratively, they build a collaborative environment where ongoing peer support and collective reflection, and thus growth, become part of everyday practice (National Education Association, 2020).

Give Staff Shout-Outs

Regularly invite educators to write notes of encouragement to colleagues. This could be via sticky notes, text, email, or a shared bulletin board in the staff lounge. These quick acknowledgments help normalize support and work to ensure that no one's efforts go unseen. Even these small expressions of appreciation are powerful buffers against burnout and boost relational trust among staff (Doan, Steiner, Pandey, & Woo, 2023).

An Appreciation Story

At one elementary school, the principal set up a small appreciation wall in the staff lounge stocked with colorful sticky notes. Within days, teachers began leaving quick messages for one another, such as: *Thanks for covering my class*, *Your morning greetings brighten our hallway*, and *Loved your lesson today*. The notes took seconds to write but made a noticeable difference. Staff said it felt good to be seen, and the lounge slowly shifted from a place of quiet exhaustion to a spot of encouragement and connection.

Provide Opportunities for Collaborative Problem-Solving Rounds

Support deepens when staff have structured opportunities to solve real challenges together, not just surface-level logistics. In these brief rounds, a teacher presents a current challenge while peers listen, ask clarifying questions, and offer possible approaches. The goal is not to fix everything in the moment, but to model the kind of responsiveness we want in our schools: listening first, then offering constructive support. Educators who experience this process feel not only less isolated, but also more capable of navigating complexity because they are drawing on collective wisdom rather than carrying problems alone.

A Collaboration Story

During a quick problem-solving round in her weekly team meeting, a science teacher shared a challenge she was having with lab groups falling apart. Colleagues listened first, asked a few clarifying questions, and then offered two or three practical ideas she could try. The whole process took under ten minutes, but she left feeling lighter and more supported, which reminded her that she didn't have to navigate tough moments alone and that her team's shared wisdom was one of her greatest resources.

Form Workload Flexibility Partnerships

Sometimes the greatest support is practical. Schools can foster *coverage partnerships*, in which colleagues step in for each other during peak stress periods—covering a class so someone can attend a child's event, trading duties during grading season, or offering to take recess duty when someone is unwell. These reciprocal arrangements signal that personal needs are not only understood but also respected. Such gestures reinforce the message: *We don't just share the mission; we share the load.*

Embrace Reflective Learning Walks

Instead of evaluative observations, staff can pair up to visit each other's classrooms with the sole purpose of learning and encouragement. Afterward, partners share affirmations and ask reflective questions. This process communicates trust and appreciation, transforming what can feel like isolating work into a collective growth journey. It also combats the silence that sometimes emerges when adults feel unseen in their efforts.

Support Strategies for Adults in District-to-School Leadership

Support is the feeling that says, "You don't have to carry this alone." When district leaders embody this message, principals become more capable of extending deep support to their staff. Without district-level support, principals often slip into reactive management instead of relational leadership.

The following sample strategies help districts build the scaffolding that makes sustainable support possible at every level.

Provide Consistent, Solutions-Focused Supervisor Meetings

District supervisors can schedule bi-weekly or monthly meetings with campus principals that prioritize coaching, listening, and problem solving. Instead of focusing solely on compliance, these meetings become safe spaces to unpack challenges, request resources, and think strategically. Principals who feel supported are more likely to support their teachers in the same responsive way.

Create Access Pathways to Real Help

Support erodes when principals are told what to fix but not given the tools to fix it. District leaders can build supportive climates by ensuring access to substitutes, behavior specialists, mental health professionals, instructional coaches, and operational resources. When help is accessible and does not require a battle to obtain it, principals learn to replicate this same accessibility with their own staff and students.

Advocate for Principals Publicly and Privately

Just as students need advocates, campus leaders need district-level champions. When district leaders publicly acknowledge a principal's efforts and defend them when appropriate, they foster a climate where principals feel safe to take risks. This advocacy makes it easier for principals to advocate for their teachers in return.

Adult-to-Adult Support Strategies Created With AI

Because your setting may require further refinement or expansion of these strategies, we've included the following curated AI prompt. This prompt is intended to guide you as you generate or personalize adult-to-adult support strategies.

> Using the following sub-emotion(s)/trait(s)/strategy of support: [insert one or more definition(s) of a specific sub-emotion(s)/trait(s)/strategy from this section: encouragement, accessibility, responsiveness, mentorship, advocacy], help me design adult-to-adult support strategies tailored to my specific context: [describe your school/department/team type, your staff culture, challenges, goals]. Please propose three to five simple and doable strategy options that fit my needs.

The following is a sample prompt and the AI-generated response. As all teams and educators should do when working with generative AI responses, we have reviewed and edited the following output for additional clarity and accuracy.

PROMPT: Using the following sub-emotion(s)/trait(s)/strategy of support: mentorship and advocacy, help me design adult-to-adult support strategies tailored to my specific context: I am a seventh-grade ELA teacher. Please propose three to five simple and doable strategy options that fit my needs.

RESPONSE: The following are five simple, doable, high-impact adult-to-adult support strategies designed specifically for you as a seventh-grade ELA teacher. Each strategy focuses on the sub-emotions of support, mentorship, and advocacy—the conditions that help adults feel less isolated and more supported in their work.

Adult-to-Adult Support Strategies for a Seventh-Grade ELA Teacher

Focused on Mentorship + Advocacy

1. **"Grade-Level Buddy System" for Shared Support**

   Purpose: Reduce isolation by creating reliable, built-in support with a partner teacher.

   What to Do:

   - Pair with another seventh-grade teacher (any subject).
   - Do a five-minute check-in twice a week.
     - *"What's one thing going well?"*
     - *"What's one thing that's heavy right now?"*
   - Trade small supports such as covering a class for five minutes, sharing a resource, or helping brainstorm a lesson fix.

   Why it works: This creates a predictable lifeline—someone who notices your load and helps carry it.

   Success indicator: You both reach out early instead of waiting until you're exhausted.

2. **"Mini Mentor Moments" With a Veteran Teacher**

   Purpose: Build mentorship into your week without needing a formal program.

   What to Do:

   - Choose a colleague you admire (ELA or not).
   - Ask for a standing ten-minute weekly "mentor moment."

- Each week, bring one question or challenge: conferencing with writers, handling a tricky parent email, or pacing novels.
- End each conversation by naming one thing you'll try.

Why it works: Keeps you from feeling stuck, accelerates growth, and builds connection in a way that feels light and doable.

Success indicator: You leave these conversations feeling calmer, clearer, and more confident.

3. **"Advocacy Alerts" Within Your Collaborative Team**

Purpose: Create a culture where colleagues advocate for each other when needs arise.

What to Do:

- At the end of each collaborative team meeting, take sixty seconds for an "Advocacy Round."
    - * Each person shares one specific need ("I need a mentor text for suspense writing," "I need behavior support for fourth period").
    - * Other team members call out how they can advocate: share materials, check in with administrator, offer a strategy, or co-plan.

Why it works: This normalizes asking for help and shows that colleagues are willing to advocate on your behalf.

Success indicator: You see colleagues showing up for one another in concrete ways beyond the meeting.

4. **"Shared Resource Exchange" With the ELA Team**

Purpose: Reduce planning overwhelm by creating a culture of mutual support.

What to Do:

- Once a month, host a fifteen-minute "ELA Swap."
    - * Bring one resource you created (rubric, discussion protocol, mentor text pairing).
    - * Leave with three to five new ideas from colleagues.
- Make it casual: snacks optional, stress nonexistent.

Why it works: This builds collective efficacy: *We're smarter together than alone.*

Success indicator: You feel less pressure to reinvent the wheel every unit.

5. **"Teacher Advocate Notes" to Lift Up Colleagues' Contributions**

Purpose: Strengthen support and advocacy by visibly naming the great work happening around you.

What to Do:

- Spend one minute at the end of the day writing a quick note (on a sticky note or email).
    - *"Your annotation protocol saved me today—thank you."*
    - *"Your calm presence during dismissal helps all of us."*
- If a colleague is struggling, write to your administrator or your team lead, advocating for support on their behalf (coverage, planning time, resources).

Why it works: This strengthens relationships and creates a supportive, advocacy-centered culture—one small note at a time.

Success indicator: Colleagues begin doing this for one another, and the team climate shifts. (OpenAI, 2025b)

Creating the Conditions for Support (Adult to Student)

Students rarely say the words, *I don't feel supported.* Instead, they show us. This might be in the form of missed assignments or unwanted behavior, or it might be part of the quiet withdrawal of a student who used to raise her hand every day and now folds into her hoodie during class. When students don't believe help is available or don't know how to ask for it, they often stop reaching out at all. What might come across as apathy is actually learned disconnection.

> A single adult who offers consistent support can radically reshape a student's sense of belonging.

Fortunately, the opposite is also true. A single adult who offers consistent support can radically reshape a student's sense of belonging. Whether it's the teacher who says, "I've got time if you want to go over this together," or the counselor who notices when a student doesn't look quite like themselves, these moments add up, and they matter.

Support Strategies for Students

Like the other chapters in this text, the sample strategies in this section are small in practice but powerful in message: *I see you, and I'm here to support you.* In a world where many students feel invisible, the presence of just one supportive adult can make all the difference. (You can find a list of the adult-to-student support strategies in the appendix, page 147.)

Offer Moments of Noticing

Small but authentic acts of noticing, such as saying a student's name with warmth or complimenting their effort, can transform how students see themselves. "I saw how hard you worked through that frustration today" is more than just praise; it's a powerful reminder that says, *I see you trying, and I'm here to support you.* Small, genuine acknowledgments send a clear message of care, and when those acknowledgments come specifically from teachers, students report feeling more supported, motivated, and academically connected (Smith, Rozek, Manke, Dweck, & Walton, 2021).

Provide Structured Academic and Emotional Mentoring

Beyond a homeroom or advisory period, assigning students (especially those who are at risk) to a caring adult who checks in regularly, asking about workload, stress, interests, and emotional well-being, builds protective relationships that feel like genuine support. These "anchor adults" can track academic progress, celebrate growth, advocate for the student, and intervene early. When mentorship becomes part of the system, no student falls through the cracks unseen. According to *MENTOR* (2021), structured mentoring relationships can significantly improve students' academic outcomes and school connectedness.

A Mentorship Story

At one middle school, each student at risk is paired with an anchor adult who checks in a few minutes each week. One eighth grader meets with the librarian, who asks about his workload, celebrates his small wins, and helps him plan for upcoming assignments. The relationship is simple but steady, and over time, the student's attendance and confidence improves—proof that having one consistent, caring adult can change the trajectory of a school year.

Implement Trauma-Informed Practices

Rather than defaulting to discipline, educators can approach off-task or disruptive behavior with curiosity, asking, "What's behind this today?" This shift invites students into connection rather than defensiveness. It also affirms that their behavior is a communication of need and they're not in trouble for struggling. Trauma-informed practices emphasize the need for relational responses that prioritize connection over compliance (Overstreet & Chafouleas, 2016). It's important to note that this doesn't mean ignoring boundaries; it means holding them with empathy. When students sense that adults are genuinely trying to understand rather than punish, their defenses lower, and trust grows. A calm redirection paired with a simple check-in such as, "You don't seem like yourself today. Want to talk after class?" can deescalate tension and model emotional regulation. Over time, these consistent responses teach students that school is a place where they are supported.

Establish Personalized Recognition Rituals

Create small, consistent routines that recognize individual students for their effort or growth. This might be a Friday shout-out, in which each student is celebrated for something specific, or a private note after a tough week saying, "You showed up, and I noticed." Over time, these routines communicate a powerful message: *You are seen, you are valued, and you belong here*, which research links to stronger school belonging and well-being (Allen et al., 2018, 2024).

Schedule Academic Recovery Check-Ins

When students miss assignments or fall behind, it's easy for them to interpret a teacher's silence as indifference. Support can take the form of scheduled, compassionate recovery check-ins—short, structured conversations that frame mistakes not as failures but as opportunities for repair and growth. A teacher might say, "Let's map out one step you can take today, and we'll revisit this tomorrow." This restores hope and communicates that adults will walk alongside students rather than simply penalize them.

Implement Choice-Driven Help-Seeking Systems

Support grows when students can choose how to access help. This could be a posted menu of options: peer tutor, after-school check-in, digital question box, or quick lunchtime review. By normalizing multiple pathways to support, adults reduce the stigma of asking for help and allow students to exercise autonomy. Over time, this builds a culture where seeking support is seen as a strength and not a weakness.

A Choice Story

In one teacher's classroom, a student who rarely spoke up in class began using the question box to ask for clarification on homework. Within a few weeks, he started attending lunchtime reviews as well. The simple menu of options made support feel normal, gave him the autonomy to choose what felt safest, and turned asking for help into an everyday strength.

Practice Strength Spotting

Support isn't only about intervening in struggle—it's also about amplifying what's strong. Teachers can integrate strength spotting into everyday instruction, noting aloud a student's persistence, curiosity, or kindness. This goes beyond generic praise; it highlights a personal quality the student might not yet recognize in themselves. When adults reflect back these strengths, students internalize a sturdier sense of identity and resilience.

A Strength-Spotting Story

During a writing workshop, a teacher paused beside a student who often doubted her abilities. Instead of commenting on grammar, the teacher said, "I noticed how persistently you kept revising this paragraph; that kind of determination is one of your strengths." The student's face lit up. It was a small moment, but hearing a quality named so specifically helped her see herself differently. In classrooms where teachers regularly spot strengths, students begin to internalize a deeper, more resilient sense of who they are.

Maintain Check-In/Checkout (CICO) Rituals

A simple, daily touchpoint at the start and end of a class or a school day can make students feel anchored. A teacher or staff member greets a student by name, asks one personal and one academic question ("How are you coming in to class today?" and "What's one thing you want to focus on?"), and closes with affirmation ("I noticed you kept working on that paragraph even when it was frustrating" or "You asked a great clarifying question today."). These rituals communicate consistency and care and show students that they are seen not only for their performance but also for their presence. Over time, these moments build trust and predictability, which are two cornerstones of feeling supported.

Adult-to-Student Support Strategies Created With AI

We recognize that you might need to adapt or supplement the previously outlined strategies to fit your unique context, or you may be seeking more. To help you with this, we curated the following AI prompt designed to support developing and customizing adult-to-student support strategies.

> Using the following sub-emotion(s)/trait(s)/strategy of support: [insert one or more definition(s) of a specific sub-emotion(s)/trait(s)/strategy from this section: encouragement, accessibility, responsiveness, mentorship, advocacy], help me design adult-to-student support strategies tailored to my specific context: [describe your school/department/team type, your staff culture, challenges, goals]. Please propose three to five simple and doable strategy options that fit my needs.

The following is a sample prompt and the AI-generated response. As all teams and educators should do when working with generative AI responses, we have reviewed and edited the following output for additional clarity and accuracy.

> **PROMPT:** Using the following sub-emotion(s)/trait(s)/strategy of support: accessibility and responsiveness, help me design adult-to-student support strategies tailored to my specific context: I am the principal of an elementary school. Please propose three to five simple and doable strategy options that fit my needs.
>
> **RESPONSE**: The following are five simple, high-impact adult-to-student support strategies tailored specifically to your role as an elementary school principal, centered on the support

traits of accessibility and responsiveness. Each strategy helps ensure students feel help is available, adults are approachable, and their needs—big and small—are noticed and addressed.

Adult-to-Student Support Strategies for an Elementary School Principal

Focused on Accessibility + Responsiveness

1. **"Open-Door Mornings" (ten minutes per day)**

   Purpose: Make yourself consistently accessible to all students in a warm, predictable way.

   What to Do:

   - Choose a daily ten-minute window (for example, 7:40 a.m.–7:50 a.m.) when students may stop by your office for a quick visit.
   - Keep it light—stickers, a high-five, a question of the day.
   - Invite students who need extra connection but allow spontaneous drop-ins too.

   Why it works: Your presence signals *I'm here for you,* especially for students who rarely seek help on their own.

   Success indicator: Over time, students use this time to share wins, worries, or needs before they escalate.

2. **"Principal Check-in Cards" for Quick Responsiveness**

   Purpose: Give students an accessible, nonverbal way to ask for help.

   What to Do:

   - Create simple half-sheet cards.
     - *"I need help with . . ."*
     - *"Something is worrying me . . ."*
     - *"Can you talk to me today?"*
   - Place the cards in a box in the library, cafeteria, or main hallway.
   - Check the box twice a day and respond within twenty-four hours (or sooner if urgent).

   Why it works: Students—especially quieter ones—often communicate their needs more readily in writing.

Success indicator: You receive consistent cards from a broad range of students, not just the ones already on your radar.

3. **"Lunch Bunch" Listening Sessions**

   Purpose: Make your responsiveness visible by intentionally listening.

   What to Do:

   - Choose one day a week to host a small-group lunch (four to six students).
   - Rotate groups by class, grade level, or groups recommended by teachers.
   - Ask two simple prompts.
     - *"What's going well at our school?"*
     - *"What's one thing you think we should fix or make better?"*
   - Follow up publicly when appropriate.
     - *"Third graders told me the swings need new seats—we're on it."*

   Why it works: Students feel seen when they know their observations lead to action.

   Success indicator: Students begin approaching you with ideas because they trust you'll listen.

4. **"Responsive Classroom Walks"**

   Purpose: Show students that support is mobile—you're willing to go where the needs are.

   What to Do:

   - Dedicate ten to fifteen minutes each day to walking the building at a predictable time.
   - Greet students by name, kneel beside desks, pause at recess conflicts, and notice positive behavior.
   - Ask one simple question often.
     - *"Do you need anything today?"*

Why it works: Students often disclose needs when you meet them in their space rather than bringing them to yours.

Success indicator: Students start flagging you down in hallways to share successes or concerns.

5. **"Help Is Coming" Protocol for Student Concerns**

Purpose: Establish a clear, reliable system for addressing student needs quickly.

What to Do:

- Train staff to send a quick message (text, email, or form) when a student needs principal support.
- Commit to responding within a consistent time frame (for example, ten to fifteen minutes, when possible).
- When you arrive, always begin with the following.
  - *"Thank you for letting me know. I'm here now."*

Why it works: Responsiveness builds trust—students learn that when they reach out, adults show up.

Success indicator: Students begin asking for help earlier, before conflicts escalate. (OpenAI, 2025b)

Issues That Transcend School Climate

If you have repeatedly come to this chapter seeking help to feel supported, you might discover that the problems you face are bigger than the climate. Repeated climate patterns are a symptom of the culture. The ideas we've shared in this chapter are meant to offer support in the here and now. These are strategies for the present moment to help you or those around you feel supported. But these tools are temporary. If behaviors around you continue to erode your sense of support, it may be a sign that what you are facing isn't just a climate issue, but something deeper that needs to be addressed.

Support and Self-Care or Educator Wellness

Everything in this chapter underscores another essential truth: Self-care or educator wellness cannot exist without support. When adults feel like they must carry everything alone, including students' needs, instructional pressures, administrative demands, and family obligations, stress compounds rapidly. A lack of support activates the same survival responses seen when safety is missing: withdrawal, self-doubt, and emotional exhaustion (Bosmans et al., 2020). Without accessible resources, responsive leaders, or reliable colleagues to lean on, even highly committed educators begin to burn out under the weight of doing more with less (Bakker & Demerouti, 2017). You cannot practice meaningful self-care in a culture in which asking for help feels risky or where support is inconsistent or absent. Just as with safety, chronic unsupported effort doesn't stay contained at school; it follows educators home and shows up as irritability, sleep disruption, fatigue, and diminished well-being (Doan et al., 2023).

At the same time, support is something we can strengthen both individually and collectively. While systemic support matters deeply, educators also benefit from cultivating their own practices of care and connection through daily habits that remind them they *don't* have to do this work in isolation. To intentionally build your own sense of support, you may experiment with any of the following strategies (Boogren, 2018).

- Schedule dates with your loved ones in your calendar, just like you would a doctor's appointment.
- Start a positive email exchange with your friends or colleagues. Every day, each person sends an email with + + + in the subject line, and in the body of the email, they share three positive things about their day.
- Practice asking for targeted help ("Can you look at this lesson with me?" or "Can we swap duties this week?").
- Join or create a professional circle—a small peer group focused on shared reflection, collaboration, and celebration.
- Engage in mentorship, either as a mentor or mentee; both roles build belonging and shared purpose.
- Set boundaries around your workload by naming what is realistic and what requires team or leadership support.

And just like safety, the benefits of support are contagious. Research shows that when educators feel supported—through encouragement, responsiveness, mentoring, and advocacy—they are more regulated, more collaborative, and more effective (Ray & Pana-Cryan, 2021; Weller Swanson & Caskey, 2024). These adults then model the very conditions students need: responsiveness, availability, and connection (Smith et al., 2021). Supportive adults help create supportive classrooms.

When students see educators demonstrate both vulnerability ("I need help") and responsiveness ("I've got your back"), students internalize that help is available, setbacks are navigable, and asking for support is a sign of strength, not weakness. In supported schools, self-care becomes proactive rather than emergency recovery. When we consciously build school climates where no one has to wonder if help will come, we build the conditions for sustainable wellness. Supported adults create supported students, and that is the heart of a thriving school community.

Supported adults create supported students, and that is the heart of a thriving school community.

Support and School Culture

When climate strategies are ineffective, and support is inconsistent or entirely absent, something deeper and more enduring is at work: the culture. In these environments, people may stop asking for help not because they don't need it, but because they've learned it won't come. Over time, this absence becomes a pattern where support is no longer expected; withdrawal and quiet resignation take root in its place.

A school culture that lacks support is rarely passive. Lack of support manifests in staff meetings where no one volunteers and in classrooms where students give up before they begin. These behaviors or lack of supportive behaviors are signals. They point to cultural norms that prioritize compliance and create an environment where educators and staff are forced to struggle silently without the support they need and deserve.

To shift this, schools must move from gestures of support to patterns of support. This requires leaders and educators to ask difficult questions.

- Are support structures available and reliable?
- Do staff and students trust that asking for help won't cost them respect or opportunity?
- Are advocacy and mentorship embedded or left to chance?

When schools address these questions honestly and take aligned, visible action, they foster a sustainable climate where support is expected, people check in without prompting, and help arrives without having to beg for it. When support shifts from a hopeful feeling to a defining feature of how the school operates, a supportive climate becomes a supportive culture.

The Climate We Create

Feeling supported is an essential need in schools. When it's present, it uplifts every corner of the school. When support is missing, however, even the strongest educators and most resilient students begin to withdraw. This chapter is a reminder that support resides in small moments: an open door, a genuine question, small celebrations, and advocacy. As educators, we have the power to be that steady presence for one another and for our students. And when we commit to implementing strategies that make support visible and reliable, we remind each other: *You don't have to carry it alone.*

CHAPTER 4

Feeling Valued

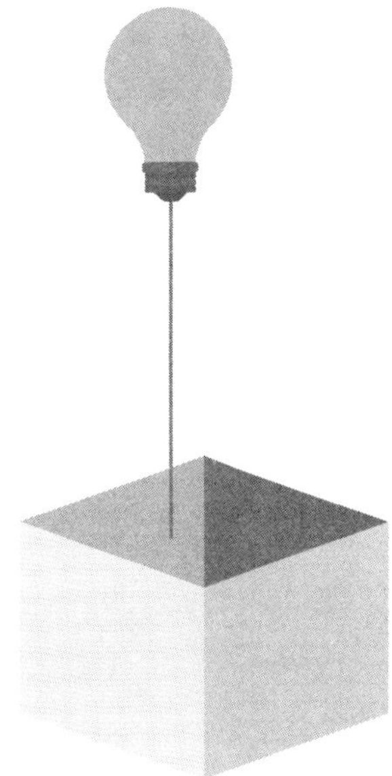

When I don't feel valued, I start wondering why I should even try.
—SIXTH-GRADE STUDENT

When I don't feel valued, the part of me that loves this job goes quiet.
—SCHOOL COUNSELOR

When I don't feel valued, it's hard to keep pouring into a system that doesn't seem to see me.
—PRINCIPAL SUPERVISOR

You're here because you want the people in your care to know they matter. You want students to walk into your classroom believing that their presence is a gift. You want your teammates to feel like this is more than just a job. You want your school to be a place where everyone not only feels safe and supported but also deeply valued.

Feeling supported and feeling valued often travel together, but they aren't the same experience. Feeling *supported* is about knowing you don't have to carry your challenges alone. It's grounded in access: access to help, guidance, responsiveness, resources, backup, and encouragement. Support says: *I'm here with you. You don't have to figure this out by yourself.* It's practical and relational. It lightens the load, helps build an even deeper sense of safety, and gives people the confidence to take risks because they trust help will come when needed.

Feeling *valued*, on the other hand, is about recognition and worth. It's the internal experience of knowing your presence, voice, contributions, and strengths matter to the community.

Feeling *valued*, on the other hand, is about recognition and worth. It's the internal experience of knowing your presence, voice, contributions, and strengths matter to the community. Feeling valued communicates: *You bring something important to this space, and we see you.* It's less about assistance and more about affirmation. Where support buoyantly carries people through difficulty, value grounds them in identity: who they are and why they matter.

The two emotions intersect, of course. When people feel supported, they often feel valued. And when people feel valued, they are more willing to seek and accept support. But they can also exist separately. An educator may receive plenty of help managing tasks but still feel unseen or underappreciated. Another may feel celebrated publicly but lack the day-to-day backing needed to do the work well. Healthy school climates cultivate both support that strengthens capacity and value that strengthens belonging.

In this chapter, we explore practical, research-informed ways to strengthen a sense of value within a school community. Our focus centers on two key relationships: the ways adults demonstrate value for one another and the ways adults communicate value to students. The strategies we share are intentionally straightforward and sustainable, and they are rooted in everyday behaviors and interactions that help people feel noticed, respected, and appreciated for the role they play in the community. This chapter invites you to engage in the important work of helping others feel valued because when people know they matter, they are far more likely to invest their energy, take risks, and continue growing.

You Might Need This Chapter If . . .

You might need this chapter if you sense disconnection—not because people don't care, but because they've stopped believing they're seen. Perhaps your students have grown quiet, perhaps the staff have pulled back, and maybe the energy in your school feels like it's shifted into something flat. These are the signs to watch for, and when you see them, it's time to ask: *Who doesn't feel valued right now?*

The good news is that the feeling of being valued can be rebuilt. It begins with how we acknowledge each other and how we follow through on that recognition. Value is the emotional heartbeat of belonging. When it fades, people don't always announce it; they simply withdraw. They disengage in subtle but powerful ways.

To perform a quick diagnostic check, use these questions to identify whether value may be the missing ingredient in your climate. (You can find the "Climate Chapter Diagnostic Tool" in the appendix, page 146.)

- Are people physically present but emotionally checked out (for example, less eye contact, less energy, fewer contributions)?
- Do staff or students feel invisible in decision making, celebrations, or everyday interactions?
- Is quiet compliance replacing genuine enthusiasm or curiosity?
- Have once-vocal contributors become guarded, resentful, or detached?
- Are big and small efforts going unnoticed long enough that people begin to question whether they matter at all?

If you can answer *yes* to most of these questions, this chapter will help you rebuild value into the daily rhythm of your school. We offer immediate *value* strategies and ideas for strategy design for both adult-to-adult and adult-to-student situations. If you have read this chapter before and understand the emotions and traits associated with the need to feel valued, you may choose to proceed straight to the strategies.

When People Don't Feel Valued

When value disappears, it leaves behind a vacancy. People may still show up, but they show up differently. Students may withdraw during class or at recess, and staff may comply, but the spark is gone. The work might still get done, but the heart behind it fades; therefore, over time, the culture begins to erode.

Students who don't feel valued might begin to wonder why they even bother. Some may act out, while others may begin vanishing into the background. Research shows that students who feel connected (who believe someone truly sees them) are more engaged and emotionally grounded (Balfanz et al., 2024; CDC, 2024). Adults experience this in similar ways. A teacher who once volunteered to lead initiatives may now avoid speaking up around others. A paraprofessional who used to smile at everyone might stop making eye contact. These aren't just mood shifts; they can be signals of emotional exhaustion and declining motivation. Research shows that when educators feel emotionally depleted, their job satisfaction and sense of professional efficacy often decrease, which can lead to withdrawal from colleagues and school initiatives (Skaalvik & Skaalvik, 2017). These moments are not signs of failure or lack of commitment; they are often indicators that someone needs support, connection, and renewed energy to continue investing in the work.

To better grasp how these emotions influence schools and classrooms, notice what unfolds when sub-emotions or traits are not present. Figure 4.1 highlights the typical emotional reactions that appear when essential support-related sub-emotions are absent. (You can find a list of all the sub-emotions related to the four core feelings in the appendix, page 153.)

Missing Sub-Emotion or Trait	Common Emotions Experienced	Why These Emotions Arise
Recognition	Frustration, apathy	Effort goes unseen.
Inclusion	Disconnection, invisibility	People feel left out of decisions or the community.
Respect	Withdrawal, resentment	People feel dismissed or minimized.
Support	Overwhelm, anxiety	A lack of backing leads to burnout.
Trust	Guardedness, silence	Relational bonds start to fray.
Appreciation	Detachment, fatigue	There's no signal that presence or contribution matters.

Figure 4.1: Emotional impact when people don't feel valued.

Visit ***go.SolutionTree.com/schoolimprovement*** *for a free reproducible version of this figure.*

When Adults Don't Feel Valued

You might notice subtle shifts when feeling valued goes missing for adults. It could be the staff member who stops contributing ideas, the leader who avoids team conversations, or the veteran teacher who once stayed late to help others who now clocks out the moment the bell rings. We can't ignore these signals.

Sometimes the impact is more visible, however. Tensions rise and voices get louder when adults begin to doubt their place in the system. If recognition is only reserved for a select few, others wonder if their efforts hold any weight at all and may turn outwardly hostile and openly frustrated. According to the Wallace Foundation, environments where staff feel valued and emotionally supported are more stable and effective (Grissom et al., 2021).

When Students Don't Feel Valued

The CDC (2024) and EdResearch for Action (Balfanz et al., 2024) both emphasize that students who feel valued by adults and peers tend to thrive. Unfortunately, students aren't always able to articulate when they don't feel seen. If we pay attention, however, they may show us. A student who no longer turns in assignments might not be lazy; they might believe no one cares if they do the work, so they stop playing the game of school. A once-outgoing learner might stop participating altogether and instead become a distraction during class discussions. It's not just purposeful defiance—it's disconnection, and it matters.

A Value Story

In a special education classroom at a suburban elementary school, Mrs. Rios made a point to highlight each student's strengths, no matter how small they might seem to others. One morning, Mateo, a student who often avoided writing tasks, placed three beautifully arranged leaves on the table during a nature observation activity. Instead of redirecting him back to the worksheet, Mrs. Rios knelt beside him and said, "You notice things other people miss." Mateo's face lit up, and for the first time that year, he eagerly wrote a sentence about what he saw. Later she reflected, "He needed to know he mattered before he could show what he knew." In many special education settings, value isn't about achievement; it's about being genuinely seen.

Figure 4.2 summarizes the potential effects on adult and student behavior when each core sub-emotion of value is missing.

Missing Sub-Emotion or Trait	Adult Impact	Student Impact
Recognition	Lower motivation	Decreased effort or engagement
Inclusion	Silence, detachment	Social withdrawal
Respect	Reduced collaboration	Defensive behavior
Support	Increased stress	Emotional shutdown
Trust	Avoidance of risk	Hesitation to ask for help
Appreciation	Disengagement	Loss of self-worth

Figure 4.2: Behavioral impact when people don't feel valued.

*Visit **go.SolutionTree.com/schoolimprovement** for a free reproducible version of this figure.*

Creating the Conditions for Feeling Valued (Adult to Adult)

For educators, whose days are spent elevating others, there's an invisible cost when their own contributions are overlooked.

Feeling valued in a school setting is all about being truly seen. For educators, whose days are spent elevating others, there's an invisible cost when their own contributions are overlooked. Over time, the absence of value wears down morale and corrodes connection. You might notice subtle signs: fewer voices in team meetings, a lack of vulnerability in collaborative groups, or a growing sense that people are keeping their heads down and their doors closed.

Educators need to be recognized as whole people. Meaningful celebrations highlight that people's efforts matter and that their presence makes a difference. They create moments of joy and connection that counterbalance the weight of daily challenges, reinforcing that schools are not just places of work but caring and connected communities. Acosta (2026) notes that, "Purposeful celebrations enhance morale, strengthen relationships, and sustain the collective commitment to a climate where staff and students feel valued, respected, and inspired to succeed" (p. 141). When staff feel valued, not just for their output but also for their insight, they show up differently. When value is present, adults tend to stay engaged and recover faster from setbacks.

The following sections focus on practical ways to strengthen a sense of value for the adults who work in our schools. We begin with strategies that can be implemented within individual school buildings—actions that leaders and staff members can take to help ensure educators feel valued in their daily work. We then widen the lens to look at the district level, highlighting strategies that district office leaders and employees across the system can use to reinforce and sustain that same sense of value.

Value Strategies for Adults Within a School

The following sample strategies are actions that reinforce the message: *You matter here*. As a reminder, these strategies may not fit all school contexts and may need customization. (You can find a list of the adult-to-adult value strategies in the appendix, page 147.)

Establish Meaningful Recognition Routines

Carve out consistent ways to recognize contributions beyond formal evaluations or quick shout-outs. At the campus level, this might look like principals highlighting staff efforts during faculty meetings or posting "bright spots" in weekly newsletters. At the district level, it could include superintendent shout-outs in board reports or spotlighting schools and campus leaders for innovative practices. Recognizing and celebrating specific educator actions beyond a simple "teacher of the month" or "principal of the month" reinforces actions aligned with campus climate and culture while accentuating desired actions for others to follow. When educators see their work acknowledged in public and personal ways, it reinforces the idea: *Your efforts matter here.*

Encourage Inclusive Decision Making

Value is communicated when staff voices are sought out and acted on. In schools, this may be done through structured listening sessions or rotating teacher-led agenda items in collaborative teams. At the district level, inviting cross-role representatives to sit on input-gathering and decision-making committees from across all departments of the district office sends a strong signal that everyone's perspective matters, not just the leadership's. These actions shift schools and districts from top-down and compliance-driven cultures to genuinely collaborative cultures, resulting in climates where educators feel like their input matters and their experiences are valued.

Practice Respectful and Deliberate Feedback

Adults feel valued when they are treated with dignity, even in critique. On a campus, this might mean leaders providing feedback that identifies strengths before offering suggestions and isolating small and specific actions for improvement. Effective feedback is intended for educators to engage in deliberate practice. Anders Ericsson and Robert Pool (2016) describe a specific form of deliberate practice designed to improve performance through focused effort, feedback, and repetition beyond one's comfort zone. Educators can also provide meaningful feedback to one another when colleagues engage in effective collaborative teams focused on sharing practices that support student success. At the district level, it could mean district leaders accompany principals on classroom walkthroughs and then debrief by asking reflective questions and offering targeted feedback. This strategy models respect for the principal's professional lens while deliberately sharpening their observation and feedback skills.

Offer Support Through Shared Workloads

Value is expressed when leaders and peers step in to help carry the load. At school, this could be teammates covering duties for a colleague who is dealing with personal issues. Or teachers might swap supervision responsibilities during testing weeks so colleagues can focus on preparing students without feeling overwhelmed. At the district level, it might mean central office staff streamlining compliance tasks to reduce the burden on campuses or suspending non-essential reporting requirements during particularly demanding times. This signals to principals: *We see the load you're carrying, and we'll help lighten it.* These actions show principals that their well-being is as important as their productivity.

Show Trust in Professional Judgment

Educators thrive when their expertise is honored. On campuses, this might mean providing teachers with autonomy to adapt lessons to meet student needs or empowering teachers to design and lead professional learning sessions for their colleagues to demonstrate confidence in their expertise and lived classroom experience. At the district level, it could mean trusting principals to tailor initiatives to their context rather than mandating identical approaches across all schools. Likewise, this could look like inviting campus leaders to cocreate timelines for implementing new initiatives, signaling to principals that their on-the-ground knowledge is trusted to guide realistic pacing and priorities. Trust signals belief in competence and strengthens engagement.

Celebrate Collective Wins

Value deepens when entire teams are acknowledged, not just individuals. Recognition of group effort reinforces the belief: *We succeed together.* This might be celebrating a grade level's improved student engagement or a department's effort in preparing students for a standardized exam. It is important to remember to celebrate entire support teams for their shared contributions to keeping the school running effectively. This might look like celebrating the custodial and maintenance staff after preparing the building for a large community event and acknowledging the pride they take in creating welcoming spaces. It could mean honoring the food service team for creating a friendly and welcoming cafeteria environment or recognizing the counseling department after coordinating a successful mental health awareness week that lifted the entire school's climate. Schools can also spotlight the front-office staff for collectively managing a busy registration season with patience and professionalism or celebrate the technology team after rolling out new devices or resolving a system upgrade that benefits students and staff alike.

Celebrations like these affirm that value is not limited to the classroom but extends to every group that sustains the daily life of a school. At the district level, celebrating collective wins ensures that large-scale contributions are visible across schools. This could look like honoring the transportation department for their teamwork in improving bus arrival times across campuses, emphasizing both drivers and dispatchers. Districts might also spotlight the child nutrition services team after successfully coordinating a summer meals program that served thousands of students or recognize facilities and maintenance crews for completing upgrades ahead of schedule to ensure safe and functional environments.

Likewise, the IT department can be celebrated for the behind-the-scenes effort of supporting all schools during statewide online testing and ensuring a smooth experience for students and educators. Finally, counseling teams across schools might be acknowledged together for guiding students through college application season, reinforcing the idea that their collective care impacts futures. These recognitions communicate that every department contributes to student success and the culture of value extends beyond instruction to every corner of the district.

Value Strategies for Adults in District-to-School Leadership

Feeling valued is the heart of belonging and professional dignity. When district leaders demonstrate that campus leaders' contributions matter, principals internalize this sense of worth and naturally extend it to their staff. District-led valuing practices are among the most powerful predictors of principal sustainability and, by extension, teacher stability (Matthews et al., 2022).

The strategies that follow aren't meant to check every box, but they *are* designed to help us remember how powerful it is when adults feel truly valued. These are small but intentional acts that remind us that our work and our presence hold real value. When we trust that others appreciate not just what we produce, but who we are, we stand a little taller—and that's what keeps us grounded and growing in this profession.

Recognize Principals' Impact With Specificity

Generic praise such as, "Great job, everyone," doesn't build value. District leaders can elevate principals by naming specific impacts, like saying, "Your work on attendance has increased student stability," or "Your staff survey shows growth in trust, and this is due to your effective leadership." These acknowledgments reinforce identity and purpose and allow principals to bring that same granular recognition to teachers.

Involve Principals in District-Level Decision Making

Value deepens when principals feel like strategic partners rather than task executors. District leaders can form advisory groups and invite authentic input, especially on decisions that affect instruction, safety, operations and maintenance, or staff morale. Being at the table strengthens principals' sense of agency and mirrors the inclusive decision making we want for teachers and students.

Shield Principals From Public Blame and Politicized Pressure

Districts can demonstrate value by ensuring principals aren't unfairly held responsible for systemic or contextual challenges. When district leaders shield principals from unwarranted criticism or stand beside them during difficult community conversations, principals feel respected and supported. This protection is a powerful form of valuing and models the dignity and respect campus leaders should extend to their own staff.

Adult-to-Adult Value Strategies Created With AI

Because every school and classroom has its own unique needs, you may find that the previously shared strategies require further modification or expansion, or you may be seeking more. With that in mind, we've included an AI prompt to support you in developing or customizing adult-to-adult value strategies.

> Using the following sub-emotion(s)/trait(s)/strategy of feeling valued: [insert one or more definition(s) of a specific sub-emotion(s)/trait(s)/strategy from this section: recognition, inclusion, respect, support, trust, appreciation], help me design adult-to-adult value strategies tailored to my specific context: [describe your school/department/team type, your staff culture, challenges, goals]. Please propose three to five simple and doable strategy options that fit my needs.

The following is a sample prompt and the AI-generated response. As all teams and educators should do when working with generative AI responses, we have reviewed and edited the following output for additional clarity and accuracy.

> **PROMPT:** Using the following sub-emotion(s)/trait(s)/strategy of feeling valued: respect, trust, and support, help me design adult-to-adult value strategies tailored to my specific context: I am a school media specialist in an underserved rural community, grades K–12. Please propose three simple and doable strategy options that fit my needs.

RESPONSE: The following are three simple, relationship-centered adult-to-adult value strategies designed specifically for you as a K–12 school media specialist in an underserved rural community. Each strategy focuses on the sub-emotions of respect, trust, and support, while acknowledging your unique role as a connector, resource-builder, and often the emotional anchor of the school.

Adult-to-Adult "Feeling Valued" Strategies for a Rural K–12 Media Specialist

Focused on Respect + Trust + Support

1. **"Teacher Treasure Finds": Noticing and Naming Colleagues' Strengths**

   Purpose: Build respect and trust by becoming a quiet curator of what's going well.

   What to Do:

   - As teachers come to the library, or as you visit classrooms for book drops, note a small positive action you observe—a clever anchor chart, a calm redirection, a creative project, or a connection with a student.
   - Capture it in a **fifteen-second email or sticky note.**
     * *"Your read-aloud rhythm today was beautiful—your students were hanging on every word."*
     * *"Your science stations were buzzing with curiosity. Loved seeing it!"*
   - Deliver it privately. No fanfare, just genuine acknowledgment.

   Why it works: Teachers in rural schools often feel unseen. When you honor their craft, you build respect and trust—and colleagues begin to see the library as a supportive hub, not just a service point.

   Success indicator: Teachers start stopping by more often—not just for materials, but for connection.

2. **"Library as Staff Haven": A Small Ritual of Care for Adults**

   Purpose: Signal support and value by making the library a calm, respectful space for staff to breathe.

What to Do:

- Set up a tiny "Staff Respite Shelf" or corner with the following.
    * A few rotating inspirational books
    * A basket of tea or mints
    * A sign that says, *"Grown-Ups Welcome: Take One Minute to Breathe."*
- Once a week, add a short note such as the following.
    * *"Thanks for all you do for our kids."*
    * *"You matter here."*

Why it works: In rural communities—where staffing is thin and responsibilities huge—these small gestures communicate: *I see you. I respect your work. You're not alone.*

Success indicator: Staff begin stopping in during prep periods just to "reset," strengthening trust and connection across the building.

3. **"Collaboration Concierge": Offering Help That Honors Teacher Expertise**

Purpose: Demonstrate trust and professional respect by supporting teachers *without* adding to their plates.

What to Do:

- Approach grade-level teams or individual teachers with a simple, supportive offer.
    * *"Tell me the unit you're teaching next—I'll pull resources that support your goals."*
    * *"Want me to create a quick book list for your theme?"*
    * *"If you want, I can co-teach the research part of that project."*
- Always frame it as partnership, not correction.

Why it works: Teachers feel valued when their time, autonomy, and expertise are respected. When you tailor support to *their* curriculum and *their* goals, you communicate deep trust.

Success indicator: Teachers begin proactively inviting you into instruction or planning because they know you are responsive, reliable, and respectful of their craft. (OpenAI, 2025b)

Creating the Conditions for Feeling Valued (Adult to Student)

You might see the lack of feeling valued in the student who used to light up during class but now keeps their hood up and their eyes down. For many young people, withdrawing is a protective move. It's what they do when they start believing their presence doesn't matter.

For many young people, withdrawing is a protective move. It's what they do when they start believing their presence doesn't matter.

Again, feeling valued is different from feeling supported. Support helps a student through something; feeling valued tells them they matter, no matter what. Feeling valued isn't just about being praised for performance; it's about being seen for who they are, especially on the hard days. When students stop feeling that way, they begin to shrink themselves.

A Value Story

In a rural high school tucked among wheat fields in eastern Nebraska, students in the agriculture science program spent weeks preparing for their spring expo. One student, Maria, had been quietly perfecting her soil analysis project, convinced it "wasn't anything special." On presentation day, her FFA adviser invited the entire school board to attend and opened the event by saying, "This work represents some of the best thinking in our district." When Maria's name was called for recognition, the applause from her tight-knit school echoed in the small gym. Later, she said, "I didn't know people cared about what I could do."

In places where everyone knows one another, public acknowledgment can carry extraordinary weight and turn a student's self-doubt into pride. But the opposite is also true. One adult who consistently communicates worth can significantly impact a student's entire school experience. It could be the teacher who says, "You bring something important to this class." Or it might be the bus driver who remembers every rider's name. It might be the librarian who saves the last copy of a book a student mentioned once in passing. These actions all say: *You matter.*

Value Strategies for Students

The sample strategies that follow offer simple, powerful ways for adults to communicate with students: *You matter here.* These are intentional gestures that help students understand their contributions, perspectives, and identities are valued. When young people trust that adults truly see them, not just their grades or behaviors, but their whole selves, they show up more confidently and courageously in their learning. (You can find a list of the adult-to-student value strategies in the appendix, page 147.)

Practice Daily Recognition

Students feel valued when they are consistently seen. This might be greeting each student by name at the door or pausing during class to acknowledge effort. Recognition should be personal and specific, not generic or superficial. A simple statement, such as "I noticed how carefully you revised that paragraph," affirms visibility and goes a long way in making students feel valued. Recognition deepens when it becomes part of the fabric of daily routines.

An Acknowledgment Story

Ms. Jordan greets every student by name as they enter her classroom and makes a point to notice one specific effort during the lesson. One morning, she paused beside a student and said, "I saw how you went back to fix that sentence even though it was frustrating. Your persistence really stood out." The student smiled and sat up a little straighter. These small, specific moments of recognition became part of her daily routine, helping students feel genuinely seen and valued.

Offer Inclusive Classroom Roles

Value grows when students are invited into the school community. Providing rotating leadership roles in class discussions or including student voices in shaping class agreements ensures all students and their voices belong in the classroom community. These small acts of inclusion prevent students from feeling invisible and affirm their place in the group. Inclusion can also be built into classroom systems that give every student an authentic way to contribute. Teachers may establish rotating responsibilities, such as discussion leader or peer coach, which allow each student to be trusted with leadership. Beyond logistics, inclusion expands when students are asked to help design parts of lessons, choose reading materials from diverse backgrounds, or collaborate on schoolwide initiatives. These practices affirm belonging and show that everyone's contributions carry weight in the community.

Encourage Respect in Moments of Conflict

When conflict arises, students watch closely to see whether they are treated with dignity. It is important that educators respond with fairness. When educators are involved in moments of conflict with students, listening first and avoiding sarcasm communicates respect, even while disciplining a student. This level of care and respect reinforces that disagreements or mistakes do not erase worth. Respect tells students that they matter even when they struggle or make a mistake. Respectful interactions during tense moments might include using probing questions instead of punitive statements, inviting the student to explain their perspective, or ensuring discipline is consistent across all students to avoid perceptions of favoritism.

Teachers who privately correct behavior instead of shaming students in front of peers, or administrators who involve students in problem solving rather than only issuing consequences, communicate that respect is not conditional. Even in conflict, the underlying message to students is that their dignity will always remain intact.

Offer Support Without Stigma

Students feel valued when receiving help doesn't carry shame. This might look like offering additional instruction without disgrace by embedding support into regular class routines or pairing peers for collaborative learning. Support affirms that their needs are seen and that they are not lesser for needing help. Schools can reinforce this by normalizing help-seeking as part of learning. For example, teachers might say, "Everyone needs support sometimes; that's how we all grow," and then provide optional review sessions, flexible grouping, digital resources accessible to all students, or appropriate accommodations. Counselors or interventionists can also join classrooms in ways that avoid singling out individual students. When help is framed as a resource rather than a remedy for weakness, students internalize the message that they matter and that their learning is worth investing in.

Promote Trust Through Responsibility

Granting responsibility communicates belief in competence. Trusting a student to lead part of a project, monitor class routines, or mentor a peer says: *We believe in you.* These responsibilities cultivate ownership and show that students' contributions hold weight. Opportunities for responsibility can be intentionally woven into the school day. Teachers might ask students to co-facilitate a lesson, serve as peer tutors, or lead group reflections at the end of class. Administrators can create student advisory councils where learners weigh in on school initiatives, school safety, school spirit, or event planning. Even small gestures like trusting students to manage classroom technology or coordinate peer celebrations communicate a powerful truth that their decisions matter. When responsibility is extended, students rise to meet it, reinforcing their sense of competence and belonging.

Offer Appreciation Beyond Achievement

Students often receive recognition only for grades or awards, but appreciation should also highlight effort, kindness, or perseverance. Notes of gratitude, quick comments like, "I'm glad you're here today," or celebrating the student who encourages and cares for their peers all send the message that students are valued for who they are and how they treat others, not just what they produce. Appreciation can be embedded in both private and public ways. Teachers might write short notes of thanks to their students, call home to share something positive, or take time to highlight effort, kindness, or perseverance in schoolwide announcements. Staff members such as coaches, aides, and office personnel can also participate by affirming students for their presence and character. Schools that consistently celebrate appreciation for effort and not just outcomes foster a climate where students learn that their worth is not conditional and solely based on performance but also connected to who they are.

Celebrate Progress and Identity

Students feel valued when both their growth and their identities are celebrated. This could be showcasing student work in the hallway or honoring cultural traditions in class projects. When students see themselves reflected and affirmed, their motivation and self-worth rise. Celebration can take many forms: Teachers may highlight incremental growth by highlighting before-and-after work samples or invite students to create portfolios that showcase their learning journey. Schools can host cultural events, include community cultural elements in curriculum and instruction, publish student stories in newsletters, or set aside space for artwork, poetry, or projects that highlight diverse identities. Even simple acknowledgments, such as congratulating a student on completing their first chapter book or honoring the anniversary of their arrival at a new school, can affirm that a school values growth and identity. These acts tell students that their progress matters and that who they are matters just as much.

Adult-to-Student Value Strategies Created With AI

We understand that your setting may call for additional approaches or adjustments to the strategies we shared. To assist in that process, we created the following AI prompt, which can help you design or adapt adult-to-student value strategies for your context.

> Using the following sub-emotion(s)/trait(s)/strategy of feeling valued: [insert one or more definition(s) of a specific sub-emotion(s)/trait(s)/strategy from this section: recognition, inclusion, respect, support, trust, appreciation], help me design adult-to-student value strategies tailored to my specific context: [describe your school/department/team type, your staff culture, challenges, goals]. Please propose three to five simple and doable strategy options that fit my needs.

The following is a sample prompt and the AI-generated response. As all teams and educators should do when working with generative AI responses, we have reviewed and edited the following output for additional clarity and accuracy.

> **PROMPT:** Using the following sub-emotion(s)/trait(s)/strategy of feeling valued: recognition, help me design adult-to-student value strategies tailored to my specific context: I am a bus driver for elementary school kids with a long commute to school. Please propose three to five simple and doable strategy options that fit my needs.
>
> **RESPONSE:** The following are simple, authentic, and totally doable adult-to-student "feeling valued" strategies crafted specifically for your role as an elementary school bus driver with long-route riders. Each strategy focuses on the sub-emotion of recognition, helping students feel seen, appreciated, and important the moment they step on your bus.

Adult-to-Student Value Strategies for an Elementary School Bus Driver

Focused on Recognition

1. **"Name + Noticing" Greeting**

   Purpose: Help each student feel seen from the very start of their day.

   What to Do:

   - Greet each student by name as they board.
   - Add one small "noticing" statement a few times a week.
     - *"Good morning, Jaylen! I love your sparkly shoes today."*
     - *"Hi, Sofia. I saw you being patient yesterday with the younger kids—thank you."*

   Why it works: Even three seconds of personal recognition can shift a student's entire morning.

   Success indicator: Students begin looking for your eyes when they board because they know you'll *see them.*

2. **"Seat of the Week" Recognition**

   Purpose: Celebrate effort, kindness, or growth, not just behavior.

   What to Do:

   - Choose one student each week for a special recognition seat up front (or a decorated seat sign).
   - Recognize them for a specific quality.
     - *"Maya gets Seat of the Week because she helped a kindergartner feel safe yesterday."*
     - *"Eli gets our Seat of the Week for using such calm self-control when things felt loud."*

   Why it works: Recognition becomes part of the routine, and students feel proud of who they *are*, not just what they do.

   Success indicator: Students begin nominating each other ("Can we pick Noah? He was really helpful.").

3. **"Bus Birthday Booster"**

   Purpose: Make students feel celebrated—even if their birthday falls on a weekend or summer.

   What to Do:

   - Keep simple birthday cards or stickers on hand.
   - When it's a student's birthday:
     - * Say, *"Happy birthday; you're the star rider today!"*
     - * Let them choose the line-up spot or do a "birthday wave."

   Why it works: Birthdays matter deeply to elementary students—and being remembered by the bus driver feels magical.

   Success indicator: Students eagerly tell you when their birthday is coming up.

4. **"Good News Window"**

   Purpose: Notice and name moments of growth that students might not see in themselves.

   What to Do:

   - Once a week, before students get off the bus, share two to three "Good News" shout-outs.
     - * *"I noticed our whole bus got quiet faster today—thank you!"*
     - * *"James, I see how much calmer you've been this week. Proud of you."*
     - * *"Aria helped someone pick up their backpack without being asked. That's real leadership."*

   Why it works: Collective recognition builds a sense of team and belonging on the bus.

   Success indicator: Students start pointing out good news about each other.

5. **"End-of-Day Thank-You" Ritual**

   Purpose: Create a positive bridge from school back home.

What to Do:

- When each student steps off the bus, say one short, kind recognition.
    * *"Thanks for riding safely today!"*
    * *"I appreciated your patience this afternoon."*
    * *"Can't wait to see you tomorrow."*

Why it works: Ending the day with personalized recognition leaves students with a sense of worth and connection.

Success indicator: Students leave the bus smiling or responding with thanks of their own. (OpenAI, 2025b)

Issues That Transcend School Climate

If you have repeatedly come to this chapter seeking help to feel valued, you might feel that the problems you face are bigger than the climate. As noted in the other chapters, repeated climate patterns are a symptom of the culture. The ideas and strategies we shared in this chapter are meant to offer support in the present moment to help those around you feel valued. If the behaviors around you continue to erode your sense of value, it may be a sign that what you face isn't just a climate issue, but something deeper that needs to be addressed.

Value and Self-Care or Educator Wellness

Everything in this chapter points to a profound truth: *Educators cannot sustain wellness in environments where they don't feel valued.* When adults consistently experience invisibility, lack of recognition, or diminished respect, the body responds as if under chronic threat, which elevates stress hormones, increases emotional exhaustion, and erodes motivation (Maslach & Leiter, 2016). Research shows that educators who feel undervalued report significantly higher rates of burnout, withdrawal, and decreased job satisfaction (Grissom et al., 2021). Without it, even strong self-care routines can feel like patchwork attempts to survive a system that continually drains them.

At the same time, feeling valued is both an internal and external experience. Being valued by others matters deeply—but so does the ability to value oneself. This is where self-care intersects with climate work. When educators consistently engage in practices that affirm their worth, such as naming their strengths and reflecting on impact, they reinforce their own internal sense of value (Boogren,

2018). Self-affirmation practices have been shown to lower stress, improve resilience, and increase problem-solving capacity under pressure (Creswell, 2013). When educators strengthen their internal narrative of "My contributions matter," they are better equipped to navigate external environments where recognition may ebb and flow.

Finally, feeling valued is contagious. Emotional contagion research shows that students and staff absorb the emotional tone set by adults (Brackett, 2019; Hatfield et al., 1994). When educators feel seen and appreciated, they show up with warmth, patience, and curiosity, qualities that directly influence student belonging, engagement, and achievement (CDC, 2024). A valued educator is more present, compassionate, and resilient. When adults feel valued, they create classrooms where students can feel valued, too. To intentionally build your own sense of value, you may experiment with any of the following strategies.

- **Name your impact daily:** Keep a running list of the ways you made a difference today, large or small.
- **Practice strengths-spotting for yourself:** Identify one personal quality you use effectively each day.
- **Seek feedback aligned to growth, not perfection:** Ask a trusted colleague, "What's one positive thing you see in my practice that matters?"
- **Create a small celebration ritual:** Light a candle, take a mindful breath, or write a single sentence of gratitude to affirm: *What I do matters.*

These practices reinforce the internal experience of feeling valued—a crucial anchor in a profession that asks so much of the heart.

Value and School Culture

When schools build consistent and systemic habits of valuing their staff and students, climate shifts into culture. As Acosta (2026) explains, in an effective culture, valuing students and staff is a non-negotiable priority and an expected outcome of how the school treats its people. A culture that truly values students and staff is one where recognition is not selective but shared, where appreciation is not performative but authentic, and where respect is universal and trust is the standard, not the exception.

When climate strategies fail to restore a sense of value, the issue is no longer about isolated moments of climate; these behaviors are, in fact, cultural signatures, the unspoken agreements about "how things are done here." In these cases, the absence of feeling valued is not a passing condition but a pattern that reveals the deeper norms and beliefs of the system. If recognition, respect, inclusion, trust, or appreciation are consistently missing, the result is individual disconnection as well as a collective culture where invisibility becomes normal.

When feeling valued is not a part of a classroom, school, or district culture, the often-unintentional message is that people's contributions don't matter, effort is not rewarded, only a few voices count, or people's opinions or input aren't welcome. In this culture, it is possible that the atmosphere can make people believe they are expendable. Over time, this pattern of behavior corrodes educators' passion, inhibits students' drive to show effort, and results in a loss of resilience and success. A culture lacking a focus on valuing students and staff can cause people to retreat into compliance and even an acceptance of failure. On the other hand, when culture fosters value in its people, innovation thrives and success follows.

If you find yourself in a culture where people routinely feel unseen or undervalued, it signals that the cultural boundaries of your school are misaligned with the beliefs needed for feeling valued. But just as unhealthy norms are learned, they can be unlearned. Growing the habits of valuing people in the culture requires schools to embed daily behaviors that communicate genuine value to students and staff. Leaders and educators must ask difficult questions.

- Do people in our school regularly hear or see evidence that their contributions matter?
- Are students and staff recognized for their strengths in ways that feel authentic, not performative?
- Whose voices tend to be acknowledged, and whose are overlooked or dismissed?
- Are decisions made *with* people rather than *for* them, and does everyone feel their input is genuinely considered?

Culture does not change overnight, but it does change through repetition. When valuing others becomes a collective habit rather than an occasional act, the belief that everyone matters here takes root. And when that belief defines the way people interact, schools move from climates where feeling valued is hoped for to cultures where being valued is expected and sustained.

The Climate We Create

To feel valued is to feel truly seen. In schools, where time is short and demands are high, we must be even more intentional about creating a sense of value.

When we build systems where value is communicated clearly and consistently, we create environments where people can bring their best selves to work. Choosing to make someone feel valued is a choice. And when that choice becomes the norm rather than the exception, our schools become more than just a workplace or a place of learning; they become a community where both adults and students can truly thrive.

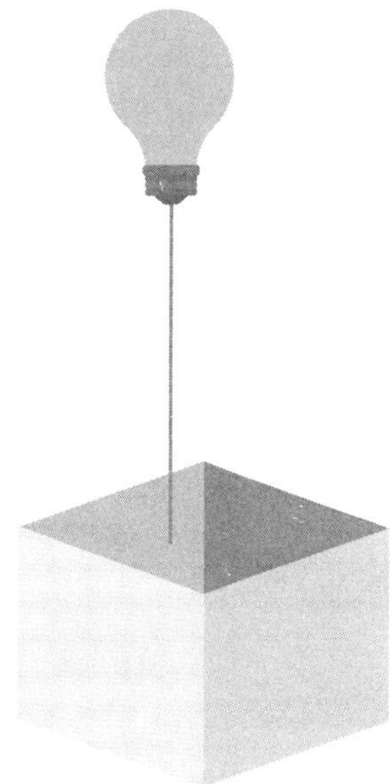

CHAPTER 5

Feeling Fulfilled

When I don't feel fulfilled, school just feels like a loop I'm trapped in and not somewhere I care about being successful.
—TWELFTH-GRADE STUDENT

When I don't feel fulfilled, my passion turns into exhaustion fast; the spark that brought me into teaching fades more and more each day.
—MIDDLE SCHOOL ENGLISH TEACHER

When fulfillment is missing, I start to question whether the work I'm doing is making the difference I hoped it would.
—ELEMENTARY PRINCIPAL

You're here because you want the people in your care to flourish—to feel energized, to grow, and to know their efforts matter. You want students to walk into classrooms believing that their learning matters and their effort connects to something bigger than themselves. You want educators to leave each day with more than fatigue; you want them to carry home the satisfaction that their work is meaningful. You want everyone in your organization to feel that their growth is visible and their joy is real.

Feeling fulfilled is not about fleeting rewards or quick wins; it is about the deeper emotional fuel that sustains momentum over time (Collins et al., 2024; Zhang & Luo, 2023). Fulfillment emerges when five sub-emotions—(1) purpose,

(2) autonomy, (3) joy, (4) pride, and (5) progress—work together to form a sense of efficacy and growth. When people feel fulfilled, they contribute with energy and lean into challenges with confidence, persisting even when the work is difficult (Shanafelt, Trockel, Wang, Mayer, & Athey, 2022).

Feeling *fulfilled* is deeply connected to feeling safe, supported, and valued, but it is also distinctly different. Safety, support, and value create the conditions that allow educators and students to show up fully; fulfillment occurs when they *thrive* within those conditions. Feeling safe calms the nervous system. Feeling supported reduces overwhelm. Feeling valued strengthens identity and belonging. But fulfillment goes one step further—it speaks to purpose, meaning, and growth. It is the feeling of *I am becoming who I'm meant to be in this work.*

A student may feel safe in a classroom yet still feel unmotivated, or an educator may feel valued by colleagues but yearn for deeper professional purpose. Fulfillment is the internal spark that emerges when people see impact, experience alignment between their strengths and contributions, and feel a sense of progress. In schools, fulfillment is the culmination of the other core emotions, but it is also uniquely its own: Where safety steadies, support strengthens, and value affirms, fulfillment inspires.

In this chapter, we explore practical, research-informed strategies for cultivating fulfillment in two essential areas: among adults and between adults and students. These approaches are intentionally simple and sustainable, rooted in everyday moments that help people reconnect with meaning, purpose, and a sense that their work truly matters. Over time, these small interactions can strengthen a deeper sense of fulfillment across an entire school community. Whether you serve at the district level, teach in a classroom, lead a campus, or contribute in a role that often happens behind the scenes, this chapter invites you into the important work of nurturing fulfillment—because people are far more likely to stay engaged, bring their best energy, and continue growing when their work feels meaningful.

You Might Need This Chapter If . . .

You might need this chapter if students and staff begin to demonstrate that they don't feel fulfilled—their sense of purpose begins to fade, even if they still feel safe, supported, and valued. Students who lack fulfillment may complete work efficiently but without curiosity, choosing tasks that feel easy rather than those that help them grow. They might say things like, "This doesn't matter to me," or "I'm just doing this to get it over with," which signals that learning feels disconnected from their interests or future goals.

Staff who don't feel fulfilled often describe feeling stagnant. They may stop pursuing creative ideas, avoid taking on projects that once excited them, or describe every day as "more of the same." You might notice them disengaging from long-term goals, losing passion for instructional innovation, or expressing a quiet restlessness, saying, "I'm not growing here anymore." In both students and educators, a lack of fulfillment isn't about not feeling cared for; it's about no longer experiencing meaning, growth, or alignment in the work.

Fulfillment is the emotional fuel that keeps people going—not because they must, but because their work feels meaningful. When fulfillment fades, people detach or burn out due to a lack of connection and clear understanding of why their efforts matter.

Fulfillment is the emotional fuel that keeps people going—not because they must, but because their work feels meaningful.

To perform a quick diagnostic check, use these questions to determine whether this is the feeling your climate needs most. (You can find the "Climate Chapter Diagnostic Tool" in the appendix, page 146.)

- Does the energy in the building feel flat, transactional, or joyless even when things look fine on paper?
- Are adults or students going through the motions, doing the minimum, or showing signs of emotional depletion?
- Do people struggle to articulate purpose, feel little autonomy, or seem unclear about whether they're growing?
- Has pride in work or learning been replaced by frustration or stagnation?

If you can answer *yes* to most of these questions, this is a good place to start. If you have read this chapter before and understand the emotions and traits associated with the need to feel fulfilled, you may choose to proceed straight to the strategy sections.

When People Don't Feel Fulfilled

When fulfillment is absent, the atmosphere in schools can shift. People show up differently. Adults go through the motions and do only what is required. Students comply but stop caring and drift into apathy or distraction. Without feeling fulfilled, the work feels empty. And over time, both individual motivation and collective culture begin to erode.

Fulfillment doesn't just disappear quietly. It leaves behind emotional consequences. Educators may feel powerless, resentful, or burned out. Students may feel disengaged, invisible, or incapable of success (Schulze-Hagenest et al., 2023). These aren't just passing moods; they are signs of deeper unmet needs.

To fully understand how these emotions shape daily life in schools, it is useful to explore the traits and behaviors that surface when sub-emotions are missing. Figure 5.1 outlines the common feelings and responses that tend to manifest when key aspects of feeling fulfilled are lacking. (You can find a list of all the sub-emotions related to the four core feelings in the appendix, page 153.)

Missing Sub-Emotion or Trait	Common Emotions Experienced	Why These Emotions Arise
Purpose	Apathy, emptiness, detachment, disillusionment	Lack of meaning erodes motivation.
Autonomy	Powerlessness, frustration, disengagement, resentment, helplessness	Excessive control undermines initiative and agency.
Joy	Fatigue, burnout, pessimism, irritability	Joyless environments sap energy and hope.
Pride	Shame, minimization, underachievement, invisibility	Absence of affirmation weakens satisfaction and dignity.
Progress	Stagnation, discouragement, self-doubt, boredom, hopelessness	Without growth, confidence falters and effort diminishes.

Figure 5.1: Emotional impact when people don't feel fulfilled.

*Visit **go.SolutionTree.com/schoolimprovement** for a free reproducible version of this figure.*

When Adults Don't Feel Fulfilled

For adults, a lack of fulfillment often begins with subtle signs. Teachers who once eagerly tried new strategies now avoid risks and stick to the familiar. Administrators who once championed new ideas now default to maintaining routines, hesitant to push for innovation without the energy of fulfillment behind them. Sometimes, the impact is more pronounced. Frustration bubbles to the surface when autonomy is stripped away. Cynicism grows when pride is disregarded. Joyless staff rooms become heavy, not because people dislike each other, but because the energy of fulfillment has drained away. Over time, these patterns lead to burnout, turnover, and a culture where people survive their work rather than thrive in it (Doan, Steiner, & Pandey, 2024).

When Students Don't Feel Fulfilled

Students rarely say the words, "I don't feel fulfilled." Instead, like with the other core emotions, they show it. A student who once lit up with curiosity now disengages, convinced their progress doesn't matter. Others may seek affirmation in negative ways such as disruption, attention-seeking, or withdrawal. When fulfillment is missing, learning feels transactional. Students focus on compliance rather than curiosity, on getting through rather than growing (Lombard, 2022). Without purpose, autonomy, joy, pride, and progress, school becomes something to endure instead of a place to flourish. Figure 5.2 shows how lacking any of the key sub-emotions can shape the way adults and students feel and act.

Missing Sub-Emotion or Trait	Adult Impact	Student Impact
Purpose	Going through the motions, detachment	Lack of curiosity, disengagement
Autonomy	Low innovation, dependency	Passivity, defiance
Joy	Negativity, exhaustion	Withdrawal, disruptive behavior
Pride	Reluctance to share, underperformance	Low confidence, attention-seeking
Progress	Burnout, frustration, complacency	Giving up easily, avoidance

Figure 5.2: Behavioral impact when people don't feel fulfilled.

*Visit **go.SolutionTree.com/schoolimprovement** for a free reproducible version of this figure.*

Creating the Conditions for Fulfillment (Adult to Adult)

Fulfillment among educators grows in environments where purpose, autonomy, joy, pride, and progress are cultivated intentionally. Fulfillment thrives when colleagues acknowledge each other's progress and push one another to be creative and innovative, leaders create space for autonomy and action research, and staff celebrate these triumphs and feel deeply connected to their purpose.

When fulfillment is present, adults persist through challenges by recovering faster from setbacks and contributing more openly to support one another and their students. They show greater creativity in their practice, collaborate with a stronger sense of trust, and remain committed to both students and colleagues over the long term. Staffrooms become spaces of energy, creativity, and shared purpose.

The following sections focus on practical ways to strengthen a sense of fulfillment for the adults who work in our schools. We begin with strategies that can be implemented within individual school buildings—actions that leaders and staff members can take to help ensure educators feel fulfilled in their daily work. We then widen the lens to look at the district level, highlighting strategies that district office leaders and employees across the system can use to reinforce and sustain that same sense of fulfillment.

Fulfillment Strategies for Adults Within a School

Fulfillment takes root in spaces where adults feel their efforts are seen and their purpose is nourished. The following sample strategies invite colleagues to slow down, pay attention, and offer each other moments of genuine recognition. When adults feel fulfilled, schools become places where both adults and students can flourish. (You can find a list of the adult-to-adult fulfillment strategies in the appendix, page 147.)

When adults feel fulfilled, schools become places where both adults and students can flourish.

Practice Impact Reflection Cycles

Once a month, dedicate ten to fifteen minutes of a staff meeting to reflect on and share specific moments when educators felt their work made a meaningful difference—big or small. This practice focuses on purpose and reconnects educators to the *why* of their work, which is the heart of fulfillment. Here's how it works.

1. The leader opens with a prompt, saying something like, "Think of one moment this month when you saw real impact—when a student grew, a colleague thrived, or something clicked for you professionally. What happened, and why did it matter?
2. Staff members jot down a quick reflection.

3. Volunteers share their moments with the group or in pairs.
4. The leader closes by naming patterns—such as impact, growth, or purpose—and linking these back to the school's mission.

Offer Autonomy in Professional Learning

Professional learning is most fulfilling when educators have choice. Rather than assigning a single mandated training, offer pathways. These might include workshops, book studies, conferences, online modules, or collaborative projects. When staff can pursue the learning that best fits their goals and teaching context, they feel trusted as professionals. This sense of autonomy increases ownership of growth and ensures professional learning is energizing rather than draining. Schools can amplify this by asking staff to share what they've learned, making personal learning visible and collective progress tangible.

An Autonomy Story

At one high school, the principal replaced a one-size-fits-all professional learning day with a Choose Your Learning Path menu. Teachers selected from options like a technology workshop, a book study on student engagement, a collaborative project redesign session, or an online course they'd been wanting to take. Later that month, staff shared one takeaway during a brief gallery walk. The energy was noticeably higher; teachers were excited about what they'd chosen to learn, and seeing one another's growth made the whole day feel purposeful rather than obligatory.

Tell Stories With Purpose

Fulfillment grows when educators have space to connect their daily efforts to the larger why of the profession. Hosting brief storytelling moments—where a teacher, counselor, or staff member shares a short vignette about a meaningful student interaction or breakthrough—reminds colleagues of the impact of their work. Sharing a moment when a student finally grasped a concept or a parent expressed gratitude can reignite purpose. Over time, embedding storytelling into staff gatherings builds a collective narrative of impact. This practice transforms routine meetings into meaning-making spaces, strengthening shared identity and reminding everyone that their contributions matter in tangible ways.

A Sharing Story

During a monthly high school staff meeting, the principal invited one staff member to share a moment that mattered. Last month, a mathematics teacher told a quick story about a student who had struggled for weeks but suddenly lit up during a small-group lesson and whispered, "I finally get it." The entire room cheered!

Offer Peer-to-Peer Coaching

Pairing colleagues in supportive partnerships allows educators to give and receive feedback in ways that highlight strengths and affirm progress. Rather than evaluative oversight, peer coaching is rooted in trust and professional growth. Teachers might observe one another's classrooms, exchange reflections, or set small instructional goals together. This not only improves instructional practice but also builds camaraderie, resilience, and a deeper sense of purpose by reminding educators they are not navigating challenges alone.

Create Joyful Traditions

Schools that embed rituals of joy into the weekly rhythm create environments where energy is renewed rather than drained. This might look like Friday coffee carts delivered by administrators, a staff shout-out board in the lounge, spirit or theme days, or a tradition of celebrating birthdays collectively. These practices signal that joy is not an afterthought but a valued part of professional life. By protecting space for levity and laughter, schools remind educators that fulfillment includes delight, not just duty.

A Celebration Story

At one middle school, Wednesdays have become Mini-Celebration Days. Each week, a different grade-level team chooses a simple theme: "favorite color" day, "silly socks" day, or "bring a childhood photo" day. During lunch, staff gather for five minutes to reveal their photos or compare their socks before heading back to class. The ritual is light and quick, but it shifted the entire midweek mood. A veteran teacher shared, "These tiny celebrations give me something to look forward to; they remind me that joy is part of why I stay in this work."

Encourage Shared Decision Making

Inviting educators to actively shape school policies, schedules, or initiatives sends a clear message: Their expertise matters. Fulfillment increases when staff feel they have real influence instead of leadership handing down decisions without consultation. This influence can take the form of focus groups, advisory councils, guiding coalitions, or structured feedback protocols before major changes are implemented. When educators see their ideas reflected in the direction of the school, they experience greater autonomy and purpose, and collective ownership of initiatives increases sustainability.

Track Visible Growth

Schools thrive when progress is made visible. This might involve bulletin boards charting collective achievements, newsletters highlighting staff innovations, or digital dashboards showcasing progress toward collective goals. Public recognition of growth reinforces pride and signals that efforts matter, even if final outcomes aren't yet reached. For example, tracking the number of completed home visits, student reading milestones, or teacher-led innovations ensures progress stays visible. By making growth tangible, schools cultivate energy and hope.

Protect Staff Personal Time

One of the most powerful signals of respect leaders can offer is honoring boundaries. Fulfillment erodes when staff continually feel like they are expected to sacrifice personal time. Leaders who commit to not accepting late-night emails, building in meeting-free planning time, or scheduling wellness breaks model that balance matters. Protecting time also includes streamlining initiatives so educators aren't overwhelmed with competing demands. When leaders honor time as a scarce and precious resource, they foster autonomy, respect, and joy, allowing educators to sustain their energy for meaningful work.

A Boundaries Story

At one high school, the principal implemented a No After-Six Rule: No emails, texts, or new tasks sent to staff after 6:00 p.m. She also created a weekly meeting-free planning block in the schedule so that teachers had uninterrupted time to prepare and breathe. Within weeks, staff began commenting on how different the building felt. One teacher shared, "I finally have evenings that feel like mine again." By protecting time and eliminating unnecessary demands, the leader signaled deep respect for personal boundaries, and staff reported feeling more energized, focused, and fulfilled in their work.

Fulfillment Strategies for Adults in District-to-School Leadership

Fulfillment grows when work feels meaningful, progress is visible, and leaders experience autonomy, pride, and joy in their roles. Campus leaders cannot foster fulfillment for teachers or students if their own work feels transactional, punitive, or devoid of purpose. The district plays an essential role in nurturing the conditions where fulfillment can take root.

The following sample strategies offer simple, doable ways to cultivate a sense of fulfillment between district offices and school sites. These are relational actions that highlight progress, celebrate growth, and reconnect leaders to what drew them to education in the first place. When leaders feel fulfilled, both professionally and personally, they lead with greater clarity, compassion, and stability.

Align Initiatives to a Coherent Purpose

District leaders can increase principal fulfillment by narrowing initiatives to a clear, unified purpose. When principals understand what truly matters and why, they feel more connected to the work. This clarity allows them to anchor campus decisions in meaning and help teachers experience deeper purpose in their roles.

Create Leadership Autonomy Within Guardrails

Fulfillment rises when principals feel trusted to lead. Districts can articulate guardrails or non-negotiables while giving campus leaders freedom to design schedules, interventions, professional learning structures, celebrations, and other campus-based practices that fit their communities. Autonomy strengthens creativity and pride, feelings that principals can then mirror for their staff.

Celebrate Principal Growth and Innovation

District leaders can highlight principals' progress through leadership showcases, reflective learning walks, principal-led professional learning sessions, or spotlights in district communications. When principals see their growth recognized, not just their outcomes, they feel renewed energy and pride. This energy translates directly into more fulfilled staff and more joyful classrooms.

Adult-to-Adult Fulfillment Strategies Created With AI

Your environment may present circumstances that call for tailored solutions beyond what we've already outlined, or you may be seeking more. For this reason, we have created the following AI prompt to guide you in crafting or refining adult-to-adult fulfillment strategies:

> Using the following sub-emotion(s)/trait(s)/strategy of fulfillment: [insert one or more definition(s) of a specific sub-emotion(s)/trait(s)/strategy from this section: purpose, autonomy, joy, pride, progress], help me design adult-to-adult fulfillment strategies tailored to my specific context: [describe your school/department/team type, your staff culture, challenges, goals]. Please propose three to five simple and doable strategy options that fit my needs.

The following is a sample prompt and the AI-generated response. As all teams and educators should do when working with generative AI responses, we have reviewed and edited the following output for additional clarity and accuracy.

> **PROMPT:** Using the following sub-emotion(s)/trait(s)/strategy of fulfillment: joy, help me design adult-to-adult fulfillment strategies tailored to my specific context: I am a superintendent of a high-performing school district in a suburb or a major city. Please propose three simple and doable strategy options that fit my needs.
>
> **RESPONSE:** Below are three simple, high-leverage, joy-based adult-to-adult fulfillment strategies crafted specifically for your role as a superintendent of a high-performing suburban district. Each strategy is designed to elevate joy in authentic, professional, sustainable ways—no fluff, no extra burden—just meaningful moments that remind leaders and staff why the work matters.
>
> **Adult-to-Adult Fulfillment Strategies for a Superintendent**
>
> ***Focused on Joy***
>
> 1. **"Joy Spotlights" in Leadership and Staff Meetings**
>
>   **Purpose:** Infuse joy into the district's professional rhythm by celebrating meaningful, real moments—not just metrics.

What to Do:

- Begin cabinet meetings, principal meetings, and districtwide professional learning days with a two-to-three-minute "Joy Spotlight."
- Invite one leader or team to share a short moment from the past week that brought joy—a breakthrough with a student, a creative teacher idea, a family success story, or a moment of staff resilience.
- Keep it brief but specific.

Why it works:

High-performing districts often operate at a fast pace. Pausing for joy resets the tone, reconnects adults to purpose, and reinforces that **impact is happening every day**.

Success indicator: Leaders begin arriving prepared with joyful moments, and the energy in meetings becomes lighter, warmer, and more collaborative.

2. **"Surprise and Delight Visits" to Schools**

Purpose: Bring joy directly to principals, teachers, and staff in simple, human ways that communicate: *I see you, and I appreciate you.*

What to Do:

- Once or twice a month, make an unannounced visit to a school with a joyful gesture.
    - ⋆ Coffee cart with cabinet staff serving lattes
    - ⋆ A "joy bag" of colorful pens, stickers, or treats for staff lounges
    - ⋆ Quick classroom pop-ins simply to celebrate—not evaluate
    - ⋆ A handwritten note to each office staff member
- Keep it brief, warm, and pressure-free.

Why it works: Your presence becomes associated with uplift, not oversight. Staff feel valued and energized, and principals feel publicly supported.

Success indicator: You start hearing, *"We love when you visit—it always feels good when you're here."*

3. **"Joy-Owned Projects" for Principals and Staff**

   Purpose: Build fulfillment by giving adults autonomy in creating something joyful that strengthens district culture.

   How It Works:

   - Ask each principal (or a district team) to choose one "joy project" for the year—something small, creative, and community building. Examples follow.
     - A monthly gratitude challenge
     - A hallway "joy wall" where staff share small wins
     - A staff book club focused on inspiration
     - A new tradition like "High-Five Fridays." Each Friday, staff take a minute to publicly recognize and thank a colleague for something they did that week, ending the week on a note of appreciation and connection.
   - Provide each school with a grant ($100–$300) or materials to bring their project to life.
   - At the end of the year, host a brief Joy Celebration where leaders share what they tried, what worked, and what it meant.

   Why it works: Autonomy + creativity + positive emotion = fulfillment. Giving adults space to design joy builds ownership and deepens their emotional connection to the district.

   Success indicator: Schools begin developing their own joyful identities, and staff take pride in contributing to something meaningful beyond required initiatives. (OpenAI, 2025b)

Creating the Conditions for Fulfillment (Adult to Student)

Students need fulfillment just as much as adults. Fulfillment is about ensuring that learning feels purposeful and meaningful.

A Fulfillment Story

For older students in a career and technical high school, fulfillment often emerges in the moments when their learning feels unmistakably real. In one welding program, a senior named Luis spent weeks practicing a difficult overhead weld that had frustrated him since the start of the semester. When it was finally his turn to lead the shop demonstration for visiting ninth graders, he eagerly stepped forward and explained the safety checks, demonstrated the technique, and coached the younger students through their first sparks. His teacher later said, "He didn't just weld that day—he lit up." For students like Luis, fulfillment isn't theoretical; it's the moment they realize their skills matter and their work has purpose beyond the gradebook.

Teachers can create fulfillment by connecting learning to contribution, allowing students to see how their work has an impact on others. They can provide choices, giving students autonomy in how they demonstrate knowledge. They can also embed joy into the rhythm of the classroom and create space for laughter, curiosity, and connection. And they can make progress visible with feedback that highlights growth, not just performance. When students feel fulfilled, they view school not as something done *to* them, but as something in which they are active participants.

When students feel fulfilled, they view school not as something done *to* them, but as something in which they are active participants.

A Fulfillment Story

At an alternative high school serving students who had struggled in traditional settings, every Friday ended with a community circle. During one of these circles, a student named Dre shared a poem he had been quietly writing in the margins of his notebooks. He read it haltingly at first, expecting laughter or dismissal. Instead, his classmates snapped, nodded, and asked him to read it again. His teacher leaned over and whispered, "You built something today that only *you* could build." Dre later said it was the first time he felt proud of something he made. In environments where students often arrive carrying academic wounds, moments of fulfillment can feel like breakthroughs, revealing strengths students didn't know they had.

Fulfillment Strategies for Students

Students need opportunities to feel successful, capable, and connected to their learning. The sample strategies that follow offer simple ways adults can create purposeful connection, amplify student voice, and help young people recognize their own growth. (You can find a list of the adult-to-student fulfillment strategies in the appendix, page 147.)

Make Connections to Purpose

Students engage more deeply when they understand why their work matters. Beginning lessons with a "why it matters" statement helps link content to real-world relevance, social contribution, or future goals. For example, showing how writing skills impact advocacy or how mathematics connects to financial literacy makes learning purposeful. These connections remind students that school is not just about compliance but about preparing to contribute meaningfully to their communities and lives beyond the classroom.

A Connection to Purpose Story

In her eighth-grade mathematics class, Ms. Patel begins each unit with a quick "why it matters" slide. Before starting a lesson on ratios, she told students, "Today's skill is the foundation of budgeting, cooking, and even comparing job offers someday. This is mathematics you'll actually use to make real decisions." Suddenly, students leaned in. One even said, "Oh, that makes sense now." By connecting the lesson to real life, Ms. Patel transformed the task from something to get through into something that felt meaningful and worth doing.

Give Choice in Learning

Offering students options in how they learn or demonstrate mastery builds autonomy and ownership. This might include giving choices in project topics, allowing flexible grouping, or providing varied formats for demonstrating understanding (for example, presentations, creative products, digital media, or traditional essays). Choice signals trust and allows students to lean into their strengths, which fosters both engagement and fulfillment. Autonomy also reduces resistance; students are more motivated when they feel their voices influence their learning journey.

A Choice Story

In Mr. Alvarez's seventh-grade social studies class, students could choose how to demonstrate their understanding of ancient civilizations: They could create a digital museum exhibit, write a traditional essay, film a short documentary, or design a graphic novel-style narrative. One student, who rarely spoke in class, chose the documentary option and produced a thoughtful, creative video that impressed the entire class. "I didn't know I could do something like this," the student told him afterward. By offering pathways that matched students' strengths, Mr. Alvarez watched engagement rise and saw fulfillment grow as students realized they had real ownership in their learning.

Celebrate Effort

Recognizing effort, persistence, and risk taking, not just final achievement, builds student pride and resilience. This can be done through verbal affirmations, effort boards that showcase persistence, or class rituals that highlight brave attempts even when outcomes aren't perfect. By celebrating the process, teachers communicate that growth is valued as much as outcomes, reducing fear of failure and encouraging students to keep striving.

A Celebration Story

In Ms. Chen's classroom, she keeps an effort board where students can pin sticky notes celebrating a moment when they pushed through something hard. One day, a student posted, "I tried the challenge problem even though I got it wrong." During closing circle, Ms. Chen highlighted that note and said, "That's exactly the kind of courage that helps us grow." The class applauded, and the student grinned with pride.

Create Progress Portfolios

When students can visibly track their growth, they are more likely to feel fulfilled. Portfolios (digital or physical) allow students to collect work samples, reflections, and feedback over time. Teachers can build in reflection prompts like, "What do you notice you can do now that you couldn't before?" Progress portfolios make growth concrete, counteracting the discouragement that arises when learning feels invisible. They also allow students to take pride in incremental improvements, building confidence and motivation.

A Progress Portfolio Story

In Ms. Rivera's fifth-grade class, each student keeps a digital portfolio where they upload writing samples throughout the year. Every Friday, they respond to a simple prompt: "What can you do now that you couldn't do before?" One student, who often felt behind, scrolled through his older drafts and quietly said, "My paragraphs actually make sense now." Seeing his progress laid out in front of him shifted his confidence. He no longer judged himself by a single assignment but by the growth he could clearly track.

Offer Student-Led Roles

Providing authentic roles, such as peer tutor, classroom helper, tech support, and classroom ambassador, reinforces purpose and autonomy. Roles communicate trust and remind students that they can make valuable contributions beyond just completing their assigned work. For older students, leadership in clubs, peer mentoring, or leading classroom discussions deepens fulfillment by showing their impact on the school community. These experiences help students see themselves not just as learners but as contributors.

A Student Roles Story

In Mrs. Hall's fourth-grade class, students apply for rotating class jobs each month: tech captain, peer tutor, materials manager, and classroom ambassador. One quiet student, who rarely spoke, volunteered to be the tech captain and helped classmates log in and troubleshoot devices. Within a week, classmates were asking for his help, and he began carrying himself with new confidence. "I like that people count on me," he told Mrs. Hall. By giving students authentic roles that contribute to the community, Mrs. Hall helped them experience purpose and fulfillment that went far beyond academic tasks.

Infuse Joy Into Learning

Infusing joy into learning doesn't mean entertainment at the expense of rigor; it means intentionally weaving in laughter, creativity, and true connection. This might include using humor, incorporating music or movement breaks, hosting curiosity-driven explorations, or celebrating small classroom milestones together. When joy is embedded into the rhythm of a classroom, students see school as a place where energy is renewed and learning is something to look forward to.

A Joy Story

In her tenth-grade English class, Ms. Nguyen weaves brief moments of joy into the rigor of the curriculum. Before diving into a complex text, she starts with a one-minute joy spark—a funny literary meme, a student-chosen song clip, or a quick debate on a quirky question like, "Is a hot dog a sandwich?" The room comes alive with laughter and connection, and then students transition into deep analysis with noticeably more energy. Over time, Ms. Nguyen's students began saying things like, "I actually look forward to this class—it wakes me up." The joyful openings don't dilute rigor; instead, they prime students to engage, which makes learning both meaningful and genuinely enjoyable.

Create Public Showcases

Allowing students to share their work with authentic audiences increases pride and meaning. Whether it's a science fair, an art gallery walk, a poetry slam, a family showcase, or a community presentation, public sharing reinforces the importance of student contributions. It also helps students connect their work to impact beyond the classroom walls. These moments of visibility spark confidence and strengthen fulfillment by demonstrating that their voices and ideas matter.

A Student Showcase Story

In Ms. Delgado's second-grade class, students spent weeks creating simple how-to books. Instead of turning them in quietly, she hosted a young authors showcase and invited families, the principal, and other classes to visit. Students stood proudly beside their books—some teaching how to make pancakes, others how to care for a puppy—while visitors stopped to listen and ask questions.

Provide Feedback for Growth

Feedback that emphasizes improvement and not just achievement nurtures both progress and pride. Growth-oriented feedback focuses on what has improved and what the student is doing well, and provides clear next steps. For example, "Your thesis statement is clearer than last time; now, let's work on supporting evidence," helps students see themselves as capable learners. This type of feedback affirms effort, builds confidence, and provides a road map for continued growth, fueling fulfillment.

A Feedback Story

During a writing workshop in Mr. Callahan's seventh-grade class, students circled back to their drafts. He knelt beside one student and said, "See this? Last week, this thesis was fuzzy. Today, it's sharp. That's real progress." He tapped the paragraph. "Next, let's layer in evidence that makes your point even stronger." The student stared at the side-by-side drafts for a moment and then quietly said, "Oh . . . I *am* getting better."

Adult-to-Student Fulfillment Strategies Created With AI

Because every context is different, you may find that additional or modified strategies are necessary to meet your needs, or you may be seeking more. To support this work, we have provided the following AI prompt to help you create or tailor adult-to-student fulfillment strategies.

Using the following sub-emotion(s)/trait(s)/strategy of fulfillment: [insert one or more definition(s) of a specific sub-emotion(s)/trait(s)/strategy from this section: purpose, autonomy, joy, pride, progress], help me design adult-to-student fulfillment strategies tailored to my specific context: [describe your school/department/team type, your staff culture, challenges, goals]. Please propose three to five simple and doable strategy options that fit my needs.

The following is a sample prompt and the AI-generated response. As all teams and educators should do when working with generative AI responses, we have reviewed and edited the following output for additional clarity and accuracy.

PROMPT: Using the following sub-emotion(s)/trait(s)/strategy of fulfillment: pride and progress, help me design adult-to-student fulfillment strategies tailored to my specific context: I am an AP biology teacher. Please propose four simple and doable strategy options that fit my needs.

RESPONSE: Here are **four simple, high-impact adult-to-student fulfillment strategies** tailored specifically for your context as an **AP biology teacher**, centered on the fulfillment sub-emotions of **pride** and **progress**. Each strategy helps students *see* their growth, feel proud of their developing mastery, and stay motivated through a rigorous course.

Adult-to-Student Fulfillment Strategies for an AP Biology Classroom

Focused on Pride + Progress

1. **"Before and After" Concept Snapshots**

   Purpose: Make progress visible so students can *feel* their own growth.

   What to Do:

   - At the start of each unit, have students spend two minutes writing everything they know about a key idea (for example, "cell communication," "photosynthesis," "gene expression").
   - Repeat the same prompt at the end of the unit.
   - Students compare the two side by side and reflect on the following.

* *"What do I understand now that I didn't before?"*
* *"Where did I surprise myself?"*

Why it works: AP content often moves fast—students can miss how far they've come. Making growth concrete builds confidence and fuels fulfillment.

Success indicator: Students begin making comments like, *"Wow, I actually get this now,"* or *"I didn't think I could learn this much."*

2. **"Protein Modeling" Wall of Pride**

Purpose: Celebrate student mastery through tangible, displayable work.

What to Do:

- Choose key models or diagrams (protein folding, operons, membrane transport sketches).
- Once per unit, select student work that shows growth—not perfection—and display it with a short label like the following.
  * *"Look how far Alex's diagrams have come; notice the detail in the labels now."*
  * *"This model shows major progress in understanding protein structure."*
- Rotate frequently so every student's work is highlighted over time.

Why it works: Publicly showcasing improvement—not just final products—builds pride and sends a message: *Your thinking matters. Your growth is worth celebrating.*

Success indicator: Students start asking, "Can you hang up mine?"—a sign that they feel proud of their progress.

3. **"Checkpoint Mastery Conferences" (four minutes, twice per unit)**

Purpose: Strengthen fulfillment by naming specific growth and next steps one-on-one.

What to Do:

- After a quiz or practice free-response question (FRQ), hold brief three-to-four-minute conferences (during warm-up work or independent practice).
- Highlight two growth points ("Your reasoning is much clearer" or "Your claim is sharper").
- Give one concrete next step ("Add one more piece of evidence" or "Tighten vocabulary precision").
- End with: *"You're getting better—keep going."*

Why it works: Personalized recognition builds pride, and a clear next step keeps progress moving forward.

Success indicator: Students leave these quick conversations noticeably energized rather than discouraged.

4. **"Progress Pathways" for Unit Mastery**

Purpose: Help students internalize progress across the long AP trajectory.

What to Do:

- Create a simple visual tracker for each unit's key skills: modeling, analyzing data, explaining mechanisms, applying concepts.
- Students color in or check off items as they show mastery on quizzes, labs, and FRQs.
- Once in each unit, pause for a three-minute reflection.
    - *"Which skill am I improving in the most?"*
    - *"Which piece am I proudest of this month?"*

Why it works: When students map their own progress, fulfillment grows. They see that mastery in AP biology is layered, achievable, and happening.

Success indicator: Students start speaking in growth language.

- *"I'm getting better at data analysis,"*
- *"My FRQs are improving,"*
- *"I finally understand this concept."* (OpenAI, 2025b)

Issues That Transcend School Climate

If you have repeatedly come to this chapter seeking help to feel fulfilled, you may discover that the challenge you face is larger than the climate. Repeated patterns of disengagement, low energy, or lack of joy are not just signs of momentary conditions; they are signals of a failing element of a school's culture. The ideas we shared in this chapter are meant to help spark fulfillment in the immediacy of the present; however, if the behaviors surrounding you consistently erode purpose, autonomy, joy, pride, or progress, then the issue extends beyond immediate climate strategies.

Fulfillment and Self-Care or Educator Wellness

Educator fulfillment is not a luxury; it's a wellness imperative. When educators don't feel fulfilled, they don't simply feel bored; they feel drained at the cellular level. The human nervous system is designed to thrive when purpose is present, autonomy is respected, joy is possible, and progress is visible (Collins et al., 2024; Zhang & Luo, 2023). Without these elements, the daily demands of schooling quickly outpace internal resources. Even highly skilled, deeply committed educators can find themselves slipping into exhaustion or questioning their impact (Shanafelt et al., 2022).

Just like feeling safe, supported, and valued, feeling fulfilled is a core emotional driver of professional well-being. But fulfillment is different because it's about meaning. It's about waking up knowing that your work matters and going home feeling that your contributions made a difference. Fulfillment is what turns long days into worthwhile days. When fulfillment is missing, the work can begin to feel heavy and hollow. When fulfillment is present, educators tap into energy, motivation, and creativity that sustain them through difficult seasons. Research consistently shows that meaning and purpose are among the strongest protective factors against burnout in caregiving professions, including education (Doan et al., 2024; Schulze-Hagenest et al., 2023).

At the same time, fulfillment is something we can cultivate for ourselves, even in environments that are still growing toward healthier climates. When educators take small, intentional steps to reconnect with their purpose, autonomy, joy, pride, and progress, they build emotional stamina that strengthens both their well-being and their impact on students.

The following are examples of how educators can nurture fulfillment as part of their personal wellness practice.

- Seek out inspirational movies, books, songs, and quotes.
- Establish a gratitude practice.
- Commit to a few small acts of kindness each day.
- Record your *why*, or your purpose, and keep it somewhere you will see it regularly.
- Infuse joy into your work every day.

Fulfillment is about alignment. When educators feel fulfilled, they bring creativity, joy, and emotional presence into their work. This doesn't just benefit them; it benefits every student they serve. Research on emotional contagion shows that students respond directly to the emotional tone set by the adults around them (Brackett, 2019). Fulfilled educators create environments where curiosity grows, learning feels meaningful, and relationships deepen. Without fulfillment, self-care becomes reactive; with fulfillment, self-care becomes regenerative.

Fulfillment and School Culture

When fulfillment is part of the culture, both students and staff connect their efforts to meaning greater than themselves. They experience satisfaction and develop efficacy, understanding that they can thrive both now and in their future. Schools sustain energy and commitment because progress is noticed, autonomy is respected, and pride in collective accomplishments fuels a deeper sense of belonging. The tone of the entire school system shifts from fatigue to energy, from resignation to creativity, and from hopelessness to success.

A culture lacking fulfillment is one where meaning is lost in routines, control is prioritized over autonomy, progress is invisible, and pride and joy are rare. Over time, these conditions stop being occasional lapses in climate and become accepted norms of how people are expected to behave in classrooms, hallways, schools, and departments. Educators begin to believe that their growth no longer matters, and students internalize the idea that effort is futile.

Changing culture requires honest reflection.

- Are staff and students given genuine autonomy, or do they feel micromanaged, restricted, or controlled?
- Do we celebrate progress or focus only on outcomes? Does growth happen in silence?
- Do we create space for joy, or do we unintentionally crowd it out?

- Is pride in one's work affirmed openly, or do cultural norms make pride feel unsafe, unprofessional, or unwelcome?
- Do we leave the day feeling drained or fueled?

The answers to these questions reveal whether your culture nourishes fulfillment or erodes it.

If you find yourself in a culture where fulfillment is rare, it signals that the beliefs and behaviors surrounding you are misaligned with what people need to thrive. The encouraging truth is that fulfillment can be rebuilt through intentional habits. Growing fulfillment into a school's culture means embedding daily practices that highlight purpose, recognize progress, honor autonomy, and make joy a living, breathing part of the work. A culture that embraces fulfillment doesn't happen overnight, but it does happen through repetition. When that shift occurs, schools stop being places where people simply endure. They become communities where both adults and students flourish together.

The Climate We Create

Fulfillment is the final cornerstone of healthy schools. It fuels the energy that keeps educators inspired and the curiosity that keeps students engaged. Without it, schools can become places of mere compliance; with it, they become communities of growth, meaning, and joy. Fulfillment is the difference between staff who simply endure their responsibilities and those who find purpose in them, between students who just go through the motions and those who discover pride in their progress.

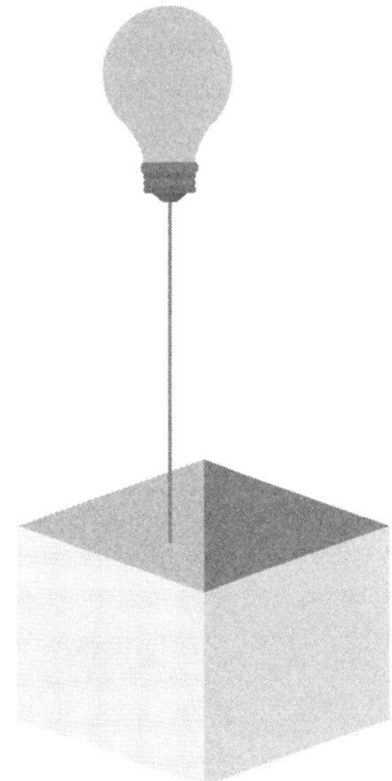

EPILOGUE

The Climate We Choose

There is a rhythm to every ending, just as there is to every beginning. As we arrive at the conclusion of this book, remember this: School climate is not static. It is not simply the weather we inherit; it is the weather we create. The core feelings of safety, support, value, and fulfillment are not accidental byproducts of good fortune or charismatic leadership; they are cultivated through intentional choices, habits, the systems we design, and the ways we treat one another.

When we began this journey, we explored the most basic of human needs: safety. We learned that safety encompasses not only the locked door and the emergency drill but also the sense of calm that comes from being known and cared for. It is the sigh of relief when a student hears their name spoken warmly in the morning, or when a teacher knows they can take a risk without fear of ridicule. Safety is not a one-time achievement; it is a daily renewal. It is the fertile soil in which all other feelings take root.

From that soil rises the assurance of support. Support whispers to us: *You don't have to do this alone.* It is the scaffolding that steadies us when challenges feel overwhelming, and the presence of mentors, colleagues, and leaders who catch us when we stumble. Support is not just kindness; it is structure. Support can be encouragement that is carefully combined with accessibility, responsiveness, mentorship, and advocacy. When schools create ecosystems of deep support, they transform isolation into a sense of belonging and burnout into resilience.

Beyond safety and support lies the affirmation of value. To be valued is to know your presence makes a difference and your contributions truly matter. In climates where people feel valued, energy rises, collaboration flourishes, and students and educators alike fully engage rather than retreat. Value is not confined to awards or formal recognition; it lives in the daily exchanges that say: *I see you. I'm glad you're here*. When value is absent, silence and disengagement spread like a shadow. When it is present, light and connection multiply.

Finally, when safety steadies us, support lifts us, and value affirms us, the deeper feeling of fulfillment takes hold. Fulfillment is the quiet satisfaction that our work has meaning and our efforts are contributing to something larger than ourselves. Fulfillment is purpose, autonomy, joy, pride, and progress interwoven into a life-giving rhythm. In fulfilled schools, educators stay not because the work is easy, but because the work is deeply worthwhile. Students persist not because they fear punishment, but because they are motivated by hope, curiosity, and the belief that they are capable of success.

These four core feelings of safety, support, value, and fulfillment are the essential currents of school climate. They are not isolated; rather, they are interdependent. Safety steadies the ground, support strengthens the scaffolding, value affirms worth, and fulfillment propels growth. Remove one, and the system wobbles. Sustain all four, and the system thrives. Together, they create what we might call the *emotional architecture* of schools—a structure sturdy enough to weather storms and flexible enough to adapt to change.

As we stated in the introduction to this book, however, climate is not only for the short term; in fact, once we understand the broader scope of this work, it becomes something we can't ignore. When the core feelings are cultivated within schools, the impact extends far beyond school walls. Consider how a student who feels safe in the classroom learns that the world can be trustworthy. Think about how a teacher who feels supported models bravery and resilience for their family members and teammates. Imagine how a staff member who feels valued approaches their community with greater generosity. A fulfilled school does not just serve its students and staff; it contributes to the well-being of society itself. The climate of a school has ripple effects that reach homes, neighborhoods, workplaces, and future generations.

And so, the question is, *What climate will we choose?*

This is not a rhetorical question. It is a practical, urgent one. The pressures on education are real; schools and districts face tight budgets, political tensions, safety concerns, and staffing shortages. These realities cannot be ignored. Yet even within these constraints, it feels hopeful to remember that climate is within our control. How we greet students at the door, how we respond to a struggling colleague, how leaders listen to feedback, and how districts design policies that honor human dignity—these are all choices. *Climate is not what happens to us; it is what we decide to create together.*

As we look ahead, there are important implications to consider at every level.

- *For teachers*, daily classroom routines hold immense power. Every time they offer predictability, extend encouragement, celebrate effort, or invite student choice, they are building climate. Each decision communicates safety, support, value, or fulfillment—or their absence.
- *For school leaders*, climate is built not only into speeches and vision statements but also into the details of scheduling, policy enforcement, and the way they handle feedback. Leaders set the tone by showing that people matter more than compliance. Leaders who prioritize emotional safety and value create conditions where staff remain committed and students thrive.
- *For district leaders and policymakers*, climate is sustained through vision and accountability. When systems measure only outcomes, they miss the drivers of those outcomes. When systems invest in mentoring, mental health supports, professional growth, and relational trust, they create climates where achievement follows naturally. Districts that prioritize climate are not lowering standards; they are securing the conditions that make high standards possible.

It's also important to remember that self-care or educator wellness and school climate are inseparable. When adults consistently feel safe, supported, valued, and fulfilled, they are more likely to remain in the profession and are better positioned to extend those same conditions to students. Wellness is not just a personal practice; it is a collective responsibility and an organizational outcome. When schools attend to the climate needs of adults, they reduce burnout and strengthen collaboration. And when educators thrive, their energy and stability flow directly into the classroom and shape how students experience learning. In this way, investing in climate is also investing in wellness, and investing in wellness is one of the surest paths to creating schools where both adults and students flourish together.

When adults consistently feel safe, supported, valued, and fulfilled, they are more likely to remain in the profession and are better positioned to extend those same conditions to students.

Just as climate and self-care or educator wellness are inseparable, so too are climate and school culture. Climate reflects the daily weather of a school—the feelings, interactions, and experiences of its people—while culture is the long-term character that emerges from those patterns. When schools intentionally cultivate climates where people feel safe, supported, valued, and fulfilled, over time, those repeated experiences harden into culture. *Climate is the daily practice, and culture is the enduring story.* One cannot flourish without the other. By tending carefully to climate, schools shape cultures that outlast changing initiatives and policy shifts.

> Climate, wellness, and culture are not separate strands of work; they are braided together.

Climate, wellness, and culture are not separate strands of work; they are braided together. Climate is the daily weather—how it feels to be in a school in real time. Educator wellness is the scaffolding that sustains that weather, ensuring adults have the capacity and resilience to shape positive conditions for students. And culture is the season—the long-term story told when those daily climate patterns repeat over time. A few sunny days do not make it summer, but consistent warmth tells us the season has changed. Likewise, when schools tend to climate with care, protect educator wellness with intention, and sustain those practices, the outcome is culture: An enduring identity of safety, support, value, and fulfillment that outlasts leaders, initiatives, and policy shifts.

The promise of this work is clear. We can create schools where students arrive each morning knowing they are safe, where educators walk through the doors knowing they are supported, where every person recognizes they are valued, and where fulfillment sustains the journey. This is not a distant ideal. It is possible now—through the choices we make today, tomorrow, and every day after.

A Closing Story

On the last day of the school year, a middle school principal walked into the cafeteria where eighth graders were buzzing with anticipation. Amid the noise, she noticed Maya, a quiet student who had struggled all year with confidence, standing with a group of classmates. Maya had failed her first mathematics test that fall, had been reluctant to raise her hand, and had whispered to the principal, "I'm just not good at school."

But something had shifted. Over the year, her homeroom teacher greeted her every morning by name, making sure she felt safe. When Maya stumbled, she had a peer mentor and a counselor who reminded her she wasn't alone. She began to feel supported. In mathematics class, her teacher displayed not just perfect scores, but examples of effort, thus valuing growth over perfection. Maya's project on designing a sustainable garden had been celebrated at the school fair, reminding her that her ideas mattered. She felt valued.

And now, on this last day, Maya stood with her friends, proudly wearing a Math Leaders badge for helping younger students in tutoring sessions. She was laughing, confident, and, for the first time, looking ahead to high school with excitement. She felt fulfilled.

The principal caught her eye, smiled, and said, "Maya, I'm so glad you're here." Maya smiled back, and in that moment, the four core feelings were alive—not in theory, but in practice.

That is the power of climate. It shapes stories like Maya's every single day.

A Final Word

The final word is an invitation: Choose to build climates that endure. Choose to design daily practices that communicate safety, support, value, and fulfillment. Choose to treat climate not as an afterthought, but as the very foundation of learning. Choose, together, to create schools that do more than instruct; create schools that inspire.

Because in the end, climate is the legacy we leave. And it is always, always a choice.

Appendix

Climate Chapter Diagnostic Tool

This tool provides a quick guide to help you identify which core feeling needs your immediate focus. Use this tool when you're unsure where to begin. Scan each set of questions. Whichever feeling generates the strongest "Yes, that's us," is the chapter you should engage with at the moment. Due to the fluid nature of climate, you may revisit each chapter regularly or find your climate needs changing frequently. This tool is a quick reference guide to enhance your ability to use the strategies offered in this book.

Feeling Safe
You may need the *Feeling Safe* chapter if . . . • People seem guarded, hesitant, or braced for conflict • Students or staff withdraw into silence rather than participate • Routines feel unpredictable, inconsistent, or unclear • Emotional tension is shaping how people move and interact • There's a persistent sense of unease, whether spoken or unspoken
Feeling Supported
You may need the *Feeling Supported* chapter if . . . • People are overwhelmed but not asking for help • Access to resources or guidance feels unreliable • Mentorship or advocacy happens inconsistently • Students or adults feel like they're on their own • Frustration is beginning to replace confidence
Feeling Valued
You may need the *Feeling Valued* chapter if . . . • Engagement is fading into quiet compliance • People feel overlooked in decisions or celebrations • Emotional withdrawal is becoming a pattern • Contributions go unacknowledged • Individuals question whether they matter in the community
Feeling Fulfilled
You may need the *Feeling Fulfilled* chapter if . . . • Energy is low, and joy feels scarce • Adults or students are just "getting through the day" • Purpose is unclear or disconnected from daily work • Growth feels stagnant or invisible • Pride and progress aren't recognized or celebrated

Strategies for the Core Feelings: Adult to Adult and Adult to Student

Core Feeling	Strategies for Adults Within a School	Strategies for District-to-School Leadership	Strategies for Students
Feeling Safe	• Protect planning time and boundaries (page 46). • Prioritize safe and functional workspaces (page 47). • Begin with emotional check-ins (page 47). • Make feedback safe and expected (page 47). • Implement rituals to create predictability (page 48). • Use shared language to navigate conflict (page 48). • Model emotional regulation (page 49).	• Establish predictable communication rhythms (page 49). • Protect principals from initiative overload (page 49). • Respond to crises with support, not scrutiny (page 50).	• Ensure clear, consistent safety procedures (page 55). • Design safe, welcoming spaces (page 55). • Greet students by name (page 56). • Build predictable routines (page 56). • Use calm corners and regulation tools (page 56). • Teach language for emotional repair (page 56). • Create opportunities for student voice (page 57). • Protect identity and promote inclusion (page 57).
Feeling Supported	• Hold weekly pulse check meetings (page 71). • Offer visible advocacy among educators (page 72). • Encourage formal and informal mentoring (page 72). • Promote openness among educators (page 72).	• Provide consistent, solutions-focused supervisor meetings (page 75). • Create access pathways to real help (page 75).	• Offer moments of noticing (page 79). • Provide structured academic and emotional mentoring (page 79). • Implement trauma-informed practices (page 80). • Establish personalized recognition rituals (page 80).

page 1 of 3

Core Feeling	Strategies for Adults Within a School	Strategies for District-to-School Leadership	Strategies for Students
Feeling Supported	• Give staff shout-outs (page 73). • Provide opportunities for collaborative problem-solving rounds (page 73). • Form workload flexibility partnerships (page 74). • Embrace reflective learning walks (page 74).	• Advocate for principals publicly and privately (page 75).	• Schedule academic recovery check-ins (page 80). • Implement choice-driven help-seeking systems (page 81). • Practice strength spotting (page 81). • Maintain check-in/checkout (CICO) rituals (page 82).
Feeling Valued	• Establish meaningful recognition routines (page 95). • Encourage inclusive decision making (page 95). • Practice respectful and deliberate feedback (page 95). • Offer support through shared workloads (page 96). • Show trust in professional judgment (page 96). • Celebrate collective wins (page 96).	• Recognize principals' impact with specificity (page 97). • Involve principals in district-level decision-making (page 98). • Shield principals from public blame and politicized pressure (page 98).	• Practice daily recognition (page 102). • Offer inclusive classroom roles (page 102). • Encourage respect in moments of conflict (page 103). • Offer support without stigma (page 103). • Promote trust through responsibility (page 104). • Offer appreciation beyond achievement (page 104). • Celebrate progress and identity (page 104).

Core Feeling	Strategies for Adults Within a School	Strategies for District-to-School Leadership	Strategies for Students
Feeling Fulfilled	• Practice impact reflection cycles (page 118). • Offer autonomy in professional learning (page 119). • Tell stories with purpose (page 119). • Offer peer-to-peer coaching (page 120). • Create joyful traditions (page 120). • Encourage shared decision making (page 121). • Track visible growth (page 121). • Protect staff personal time (page 121).	• Align initiatives to a coherent purpose (page 122). • Create leadership autonomy within guardrails (page 122). • Celebrate principal growth and innovation (page 122).	• Make connections to purpose (page 127). • Give choice in learning (page 127). • Celebrate effort (page 128). • Create progress portfolios (page 129). • Offer student-led roles (page 129). • Infuse joy into learning (page 130). • Create public showcases (page 130). • Provide feedback for growth (page 131).

page 3 of 3

A Simple Climate Implementation Protocol

The following protocol is intended for use by any educator needing a practical guide for building a climate plan using the four core feelings shared in this book. A strong climate plan should be simple and easy to manage. Whether you are a veteran educator or a new teacher, principal, or district leader, the core work is the same: Identify what people are feeling, plan intentional responses, take actionable steps, monitor the change, and adjust with care. The following protocol walks you through this process using the four core feelings—safety, support, value, and fulfillment—which, together, form the *emotional architecture* of a healthy classroom, school, or district climate.

1. IDENTIFY: What Are People Feeling Right Now?
Diagnostic Prompts • **Safety:** Do adults and students feel physically and emotionally safe in classrooms, hallways, meetings, schools, and district offices? • **Support:** Do people feel like they have access to help, time, tools, and guidance when they need it? • **Value:** Do teachers, staff, and students feel seen, appreciated, and included in decisions? • **Fulfillment:** Do people feel purpose, progress, joy, and pride in their work or learning?
Data Sources (Non-Exhaustive Examples) • Quick pulse surveys • Informal conversations • Observational walkthroughs • Teacher conversations ("What feels hard? What feels steady?") • Principal or district leader check-ins ("What's pulling on you most right now?")
Goal: Name the current emotional landscape before jumping to solutions.
2. PLAN: What Intentional Actions Will Strengthen the Four Core Feelings?
Planning Prompts • Which feeling needs attention first? (Consider the inherent need for safety first.) • What sub-emotions or traits are missing? • What is one change that would make the biggest difference quickly? • For teachers (especially new): What support structure or routine will help them feel steady this week? • For leaders (especially new): What message or behavior will signal steadiness and clarity?

Plan Priorities • Choose one to two actions per feeling at most. • Keep actions small, specific, and doable within ten school days. • Decide what evidence will show improvement.
Goal: Create a short, realistic plan, not a long list of aspirations.
3. DO: Take Deliberate, Visible Action

Action Prompts (Guidance for Actions Needed in Each of the Four Core Feelings)
• **Safety:**
  ▪ Clarify expectations or routines (classrooms, hallway, meetings, communication).
  ▪ Establish predictability (schedule, norms, or communication rhythm).
• **Support:**
  ▪ Remove one barrier (access to help, materials, time).
  ▪ Create a place for staff and students to ask for support without stigma.
• **Value:**
  ▪ Notice and name specific strengths publicly.
  ▪ Invite authentic voice into a decision or process.
• **Fulfillment:**
  ▪ Highlight progress (individual or collective).
  ▪ Align tasks and goals to purpose ("Why this matters").

For New Teachers • Pair with a mentor; provide a protected planning block. • Give one small win to build confidence early.
For New Leaders (Campus or District) • Demonstrate calm, clarity, and follow-through. • Make one visible improvement in the first thirty days.
Goal: Actions should be felt immediately, not someday.
4. MONITOR: Is the Climate Shifting in the Direction We Hoped?
Monitoring Prompts (Non-Exhaustive Examples) • Are classroom interactions calmer? • Are hallway interactions calmer? • Are teachers reaching out sooner? • Are fewer students avoiding class or shutting down? • Do new teachers appear more confident and less isolated? • Do principals report clearer communication and better emotional bandwidth? • Has the temperature of team meetings changed?

Methods (Non-Exhaustive Examples)
Methods (Non-Exhaustive Examples) • Thirty-second exit tickets • One-word check-ins • Short weekly principal or teacher pulse polls • Listening sessions or walkthroughs
Goal: Look for emotional movement, not perfection.
5. ADJUST: What Needs to Be Refined, Expanded, or Stopped?
Adjustment Prompts • Which actions worked? What evidence do we have? • Which actions felt forced, confusing, or too big? • What needs more time? More clarity? More modeling? • Where do new teachers still need scaffolding? • Where do new leaders still need support or clarity? • Which of the four feelings is still weakest, and what's the next small move?
Adjustment Actions • Scale back what isn't working. • Double down on what is working. • Introduce one new action only when the previous one is steady. • Reassess every six to nine weeks.
Goal: Continuous improvement, not constant change.

Note:

- A climate plan is less about creating a perfect system and more about creating consistent emotional conditions where people feel safe enough to try, supported enough to grow, valued enough to stay engaged, and fulfilled enough to strive for personal excellence.
- Small actions done with care and consistency reshape the emotional texture of a classroom, school, or district—one moment at a time.

page 3 of 3

Sub-Emotions or Traits of the Core Feelings

Feeling Safe	Feeling Supported	Feeling Valued	Feeling Fulfilled
Trust	Encouragement	Recognition	Purpose
Belonging	Accessibility	Inclusion	Autonomy
Respect	Responsiveness	Respect	Joy
Predictability	Mentorship	Support	Pride
Inclusion	Advocacy	Trust	Progress
Calm		Appreciation	

References and Resources

321 Insight. (n.d.). *Emotional self-care for teachers*. Accessed at www.321insight.com/emotional-self-care-for-teachers on December 10, 2025.

Acosta, M. I. (2026). *The schools our students deserve: A comprehensive framework for shaping exceptional school culture*. Marzano Resources.

Allen, K.-A., Greenwood, C. J., Berger, E., Patlamazoglou, L., Reupert, A., Wurf, G., May, F. S., O'Connor, M., Sanson, A., Olsson, C. A., & Letcher, P. (2024). Adolescent school belonging and mental health outcomes in young adulthood: Findings from a multi-wave prospective cohort study. *School Mental Health*, *16*, 149–160. https://doi.org/10.1007/s12310-023-09626-6

Allen, K.-A., Kern, M. L., Vella-Brodrick, D., Hattie, J., & Waters, L. (2018). What schools need to know about fostering school belonging: A meta-analysis. *Educational Psychology Review*, *30*(1), 1–34. https://doi.org/10.1007/s10648-016-9389-8

American Psychological Association. (2023). *2023 Work in America™ survey: Workplaces as engines of psychological health and well-being*. Accessed at www.apa.org/pubs/reports/work-in-america/2023-workplace-health-well-being on December 9, 2025.

American Psychological Association. (2024, June). *Psychological safety in the changing workplace: Work in America™ 2024 report*. Accessed at www.apa.org/pubs/reports/work-in-america/2024/psychological-safety on December 9, 2025.

Arslan, N., Arslan, S., Kartol, A., & Akcaalan, M. (2024). The predicting role of science motivation on the social emotional learning. *International Journal of Learning and Change*, *16*(5), 552–571.

Asif, S., & Shahbaz, M. S. (2025). Project success through organizational climate and work behavior: Systematic literature review. *Journal of Organizational Behavior Research*, *10*(1), 1–14. https://doi.org/10.51847/cUhkprt6DJ

The Aspen Institute. (2021). *Creating conditions for student success: A policymakers' school climate playbook*. Author. Accessed at www.aspeninstitute.org/wp-content/uploads/2021/01/Aspen-Institute-School-Climate-Playbook-Final.pdf on December 11, 2025.

Bakker, A. B., & Demerouti, E. (2017). Job demands–resources theory: Taking stock and looking forward. *Journal of Occupational Health Psychology*, *22*(3), 273–285. https://doi.org/10.1037/ocp0000056

Balfanz, R., Jerabek, A., Payne, K., & Scala, J. (2024). *Strengthening school connectedness to increase student success* (Brief No. 29). EdResearch for Action. Accessed at https://edresearchforaction.org/wp-content/uploads/55011-EdResearch-School-Connectedness-Brief-29-REV.pdf on December 9, 2025.

Ball, D. (2025, January 28). *What action steps can schools take to improve teacher retention?* [Blog post]. Accessed at www.theadac.com/what-action-steps-can-schools-take-to-improve-teacher-retention on December 9, 2025.

Bambrick-Santoyo, P. (2025). *Get better faster 2.0: A 90-day plan for coaching new teachers.* John Wiley & Sons.

Banwo, B. O., Khalifa, M., & Seashore Louis, K. (2022). Exploring trust: Culturally responsive and positive school leadership. *Journal of Educational Administration, 60*(3), 323–339.

Baumann, D., & Ruch, W. (2022). Measuring what counts in life: The development and initial validation of the Fulfilled Life Scale (FLS). *Frontiers in Psychology, 12,* Article 795931. https://doi.org/10.3389/fpsyg.2021.795931

Boogren, T. H. (2018). *Take time for you: Self-care action plans for educators.* Solution Tree Press.

Boogren, T. H. (2020). *180 days of self-care for busy educators.* Solution Tree Press.

Bosmans, G., Bakermans-Kranenburg, M. J., Vervliet, B., Verhees, M. W. F. T., & van IJzendoorn, M. H. (2020). A learning theory of attachment: Unraveling the black box of attachment development. *Neuroscience and Biobehavioral Reviews, 113,* 287–298. https://doi.org/10.1016/j.neubiorev.2020.03.014

Brackett, M. (2019). *Permission to feel: Unlocking the power of emotions to help our kids, ourselves, and our society thrive.* Celadon Books.

Brown, B. (2018). *Dare to lead: Brave work, tough conversations, whole hearts.* Random House.

Centers for Disease Control and Prevention (CDC). (2024, November 18). *School connectedness helps students thrive.* Accessed at www.cdc.gov/youth-behavior/school-connectedness on December 9, 2025.

Cipriano, C., Naples, L. H., Eveleigh, A., Cook, A., Funaro, M., Cassidy, C., et al. (2023). A systematic review of student disability and race representation in universal school-based social and emotional learning interventions for elementary school students. *Review of Educational Research, 93*(1), 73–102. https://doi.org/10.3102/00346543221094079

Clausen, N. R., Abouarabi, Y. B., Chen, J., Hansen, S., Velmurugan, G., Fink, T., et al. (2025). First-year university students' perspectives on their psychological safety in PBL teams. *Education Sciences, 15*(2), Article 236. https://doi.org/10.3390/educsci15020236

Clemente, J. M., Kilag, O. K. T., Ypon, A. Q., Groenewald, E. S., Groenewald, C. A., & Ubay, R. G. (2024). Enhancing mathematics self-efficacy: Intervention strategies and effectiveness–A systematic review. *International Multidisciplinary Journal of Research for Innovation, Sustainability, and Excellence, 1*(2), 274–280.

Collaborative for Academic, Social, and Emotional Learning (CASEL). (2020). *CASEL's SEL framework: What are the core competence areas and where are they promoted?* Author. Accessed at https://casel.org/casel-sel-framework-11-2020/?view=1 on December 9, 2025.

Collie, R. J., & Martin, A. J. (2017). Teachers' sense of adaptability: Examining links with perceived autonomy support, teachers' psychological functioning, and students' numeracy achievement. *Learning and Individual Differences, 55,* 29–39.

Collins, R. T., II, Schadler, A., Huang, H., Day, S. B., & Bauer, J. A. (2024). Impact of burnout and professional fulfillment on intent to leave among pediatric physicians: The findings of a quality improvement initiative. *BMC Health Services Research, 24,* Article 434. https://doi.org/10.1186/s12913-024-10842-2

Colorado Office of the Attorney General. (2025, March 11). *Safe2Tell reports rise 12% in February as students speak up about bullying, mental health, and school safety.* Accessed at https://coag.gov/2025/safe2tell-report-february-2025 on December 9, 2025.

Cook, C. R., Lyon, A. R., Kubergovic, D., Browning Wright, D., & Zhang, Y. (2015). A supportive beliefs intervention to facilitate the implementation of evidence-based practices within a multi-tiered system of supports. *School Mental Health, 7*(1), 49–60. https://doi.org/10.1007/s12310-014-9139-3

Creswell, J. D., Dutcher, J. M., Klein, W. M. P., Harris, P. R., & Levine, J. M. (2013). Self-affirmation improves problem-solving under stress. *PLoS ONE, 8*(5), e62593. https://doi.org/10.1371/journal.pone.0062593

Cronqvist, M. (2024). Enhanced student joy in learning environment; understanding and influencing the process. *European Journal of Education, 59*(3), Article e12671. https://doi.org/10.1111/ejed.12671

Damon, W., Menon, J., & Bronk, K. C. (2003). The development of purpose during adolescence. In J. L. Furrow & L. M. Wagener (Eds.), *Beyond the self: Perspectives on identity and transcendence among youth: A special issue of applied developmental science* (pp. 119–128). Routledge.

Darling-Hammond, L., & Cook-Harvey, C. M. (2018). *Educating the whole child: Improving school climate to support student success.* Learning Policy Institute. Accessed at https://learningpolicyinstitute.org/media/547/download?inline&file=Educating_Whole_Child_REPORT.pdf on December 9, 2025.

Darling-Hammond, L., Schachner, A., & Edgerton, A. K. (2020). *Restarting and reinventing school: Learning in the time of COVID and beyond.* Learning Policy Institute. Accessed on https://learningpolicyinstitute.org/sites/default/files/product-files/Restart_Reinvent_Schools_COVID_Priority2_Distance_Learning.pdf on March 27, 2026.

Dedering, K., & Pietsch, M. (2025). School leader trust and collective teacher innovativeness: on individual and organisational ambidexterity's mediating role. *Educational Review, 77*(2), 351–380.

DeWitt, P. (2016, January 26). Only 46% of students feel valued in their school. *Education Week.* Accessed at www.edweek.org/education/opinion-only-46-of-students-feel-valued-in-their-school/2016/01 on December 9, 2025.

Dirks, K. T., & de Jong, B. (2022). Trust within the workplace: A review of two waves of research and a glimpse of the third. *Annual Review of Organizational Psychology and Organizational Behavior, 9,* 247–276.

Doan, S., Steiner, E. D., & Pandey, R. (2024). *Teacher well-being and intentions to leave in 2024: Findings from the 2024 State of the American Teacher survey* (Report No. RR-A1108-12). RAND. Accessed at www.rand.org/pubs/research_reports/RRA1108-12.html on December 9, 2025.

Doan, S., Steiner, E. D., Pandey, R., & Woo, A. (2023). *Teacher wellbeing and intentions to leave: Findings from the 2023 State of the American Teacher survey* (Report No. RRA11088). RAND. Accessed at www.rand.org/pubs/research_reports/RRA1108-8.html on December 9, 2025.

Dreer-Goethe, B. (2025). The impact of mentor support and high-quality connections on student teachers' psychological safety and engagement during practicum. *Frontiers in Education, 10*, Article 1499749. https://doi.org/10.3389/feduc.2025.1499749

Dunavete, A. (2024, September 11). *The power of predictability in the workplace* [Blog post]. Accessed at www.yarooms.com/blog/predictability-in-the-workplace on December 9, 2025.

Easterbrook, M. J., Harris, P. R., & Sherman, D. K. (2021). Self-affirmation theory in educational contexts. *Journal of Social Issues, 77*(3), 683–701. https://doi.org/10.1111/josi.12459

Einav, M., Confino, D., Geva, N., & Margalit, M. (2024). Teachers' burnout—The role of social support, gratitude, hope, entitlement and loneliness. *International Journal of Applied Positive Psychology, 9*(2), 827–849. https://doi.org/10.1007/s41042-024-00154-5

Engels, M. C., Spilt, J., Denies, K., & Verschueren, K. (2021). The role of affective teacher-student relationships in adolescents' school engagement and achievement trajectories. *Learning and Instruction, 75*, Article 101485. https://doi.org/10.1016/j.learninstruc.2021.101485

Ericsson, A., & Pool, R. (2016). *Peak: Secrets from the new science of expertise.* Houghton Mifflin Harcourt.

Evers, A. T., Verboon, P., van Ruysseveldt, J., Vermeulen, M., & Kreijns, K. (2023). Teacher autonomy for professional development at work: A longitudinal study. *International Journal of Human Resources Development and Management, 23*(2), 139–159. https://doi.org/10.1504/IJHRDM.2023.10056972

Fernet, C., Morin, A. J. S., Mueller, M. B., Gillet, N., & Austin, S. (2023). Psychological need satisfaction across work and personal life: An empirical test of a comprehensive typology. *Frontiers in Psychology, 14*, Article 1216450. https://doi.org/10.3389/fpsyg.2023.1216450

Gallup. (2023). *State of the global workplace 2023 report.* Gallup. Accessed at https://advisor.visualcapitalist.com/wp-content/uploads/2023/06/state-of-the-global-workplace-2023-download.pdf on March 6, 2026.

Grissom, J. A., Egalite, A. J., & Lindsay, C. A. (2021). *How principals affect students and schools: A systematic synthesis of two decades of research.* Wallace Foundation. Accessed at https://wallacefoundation.org/sites/default/files/2023-09/How-Principals-Affect-Students-and-Schools.pdf on December 10, 2025.

Gruenert, S., & Whitaker, T. (2024). *School culture rewired: Toward a more positive and productive school for all.* ASCD.

H. B. 7009, 185th Gen. Assemb., Reg. Sess. (Conn. 2025). Accessed at www.cga.ct.gov/asp/CGABillStatus/cgabillstatus.asp?selBillType=Bill&bill_num=HB7009 on April 6, 2026.

Hall, A. J., Goodwin, V. A., Allchurch, L., Capon, L., Farrell, V., Olufunmilayo, O., et al. (2024). Feeling valued at work: A qualitative exploration of allied health profession support workers. *BMC Health Services Research, 24*(1), Article 1511.

Hallam, K. T., Popovic, N., & Karimi, L. (2023). Identifying the key elements of psychologically safe workplaces in healthcare settings. *Brain Sciences, 13*(10), Article 1450.

Han, S., Liu, D., & Lv, Y. (2022). The influence of psychological safety on students' creativity in project-based learning: The mediating role of psychological empowerment. *Frontiers in Psychology, 13*, Article 865123. https://doi.org/10.3389/fpsyg.2022.865123

Hanley, M., Khairat, M., Taylor, K., Wilson, R., Cole-Fletcher, R., & Riby, D. M. (2017). Classroom displays—Attraction or distraction? Evidence of impact on attention and learning from children with and without autism. *Developmental Psychology, 53*(7), 1265–1275. https://doi.org/10.1037/dev0000271

Hatfield, E., Cacioppo, J. T., & Rapson, R. L. (1994). *Emotional contagion*. Cambridge University Press.

Hattie, J., & Clarke, S. (2019). *Visible learning: Feedback*. Routledge.

Hecht, C. A., Bryan, C. J., & Yeager, D. S. (2023). A values-aligned intervention fosters growth mindset–supportive teaching and reduces inequality in educational outcomes. *Proceedings of the National Academy of Sciences, 120*(25), e2210704120. https://doi.org/10.1073/pnas.2210704120

Heilman, E. E. (2025). Supporting Gen Z teachers' emotional well-being. *Kappan, 107*(1–2), 13–18.

Hernández, L. E., & Darling-Hammond, L. (2022). *Creating identity-safe schools and classrooms*. Learning Policy Institute. https://doi.org/10.54300/165.102

Herr, R. M., Brokmeier, L., Baron, B. N., Mauss, D., & Fischer, J. E. (2023). The longitudinal directional associations of meaningful work with mental well-being—Initial findings from an exploratory investigation. *BMC Psychology, 11*, Article 325. https://doi.org/10.1186/s40359-023-01308-x

Hoffman, M. (2023, January 15). *Lencioni's five dysfunctions of a team model*. Accessed at https://eq4c.com/lencionis-five-dysfunctions-of-a-team-model/ on April 1, 2026.

Holland, K. (2025, April 18). *Amygdala hijack: When emotion takes over*. Accessed at www.healthline.com/health/stress/amygdala-hijack on December 10, 2025.

Hsueh, J., Condliffe, B., Corrin, W., Steimle, S., Balu, R., Hennessy, M., et al. (2021). Building toward effectiveness. *The Future of Children, 31*(1), 161–168. https://dx.doi.org/10.1353/foc.2021.0005

Hurt, K., & Dye, D. (2025, May 19). *How to foster psychological safety in training (and build a courageous learning culture)*. Accessed at https://letsgrowleaders.com/2025/05/19/psychological-safety-in-training on December 10, 2025.

Ibrahim, S., Kiran, S., Usman Dar, M., & Mahnaz, W. (2025). Situational handling and emergency preparedness in schools: A study of students' perceptions and readiness. *Journal for Social Science Archives, 3*(2), 1–21. Accessed at www.researchgate.net/publication/390480592_Situational_Handling_and_Emergency_Preparedness_in_Schools_A_Study_of_Students%27_Perceptions_and_Readiness on December 10, 2025.

Imad, M. (2022). Teaching to empower: Leveraging the neuroscience of now to help students become self-regulated learners. *Journal of Undergraduate Neuroscience Education, 20*(2), A254–A262. Accessed at https://pubmed.ncbi.nlm.nih.gov/38323061 on December 10, 2025.

Immordino-Yang, M. H., Darling-Hammond, L., & Krone, C. (2018). *The brain basis for integrated social, emotional, and academic development: How emotions and social relationships drive learning* [Research brief]. The Aspen Institute. Accessed at www.aspeninstitute.org/wp-content/uploads/2025/05/Aspen_research_FINAL_web.pdf on December 10, 2025.

Immordino-Yang, M. H., Darling-Hammond, L., & Krone, C. R. (2019). Nurturing nature: How brain development is inherently social and emotional, and what this means for education. *Educational Psychologist, 54*(3), 185–204. https://doi.org/10.1080/00461520.2019.1633924

Irwin, V., Wang, K., Cui, J., & Thompson, A. (2021). *Report on indicators of school crime and safety: 2020.* National Center for Education Statistic at IES. Accessed at https://nces.ed.gov/pubs2021/2021092.pdf on March 9, 2026.

Jagers, R. J., Rivas-Drake, D., & Borowski, T. (2018). *Equity and social and emotional learning: A cultural analysis.* Collaborative for Academic, Social, and Emotional Learning (CASEL). Accessed at https://drc.casel.org/uploads/sites/3/2019/02/Equity-Social-and-Emotional-Learning-A-Cultural-Analysis.pdf on December 10, 2025.

Jardinez, M. J., & Natividad, L. R. (2024). The advantages and challenges of inclusive education: Striving for equity in the classroom. *Shanlax International Journal of Education, 12*(2), 57–65. https://doi.org/10.34293/education.v12i2.7182

Jennings, P. A. (2015). *Mindfulness for teachers: Simple skills for peace and productivity in the classroom.* Norton.

Jennings, P. A. (2019). *The trauma-sensitive classroom: Building resilience with compassionate teaching.* Norton.

Jeno, L. M., Nylehn, J., Hole, T. N., Raaheim, A., Velle, G., & Vandvik, V. (2023). Motivational determinants of students' academic functioning: The role of autonomy-support, autonomous motivation, and perceived competence. *Scandinavian Journal of Educational Research, 67*(2), 194–211. https://doi.org/10.1080/00313831.2021.1990125

Jolly, P. M., Kong, D. T., & Kim, K. Y. (2021). Social support at work: An integrative review. *Journal of Organizational Behavior, 42*(2), 229–251.

Jones, S. M., McGarrah, M. W., & Kahn, J. (2019). Social and emotional learning: A principled science of human development in context. *Educational Psychologist, 54*(3), 129–143. https://doi.org/10.1080/00461520.2019.1625776

Kadović, M., Mikšić, Š., & Lovrić, R. (2023). Ability of emotional regulation and control as a stress predictor in healthcare professionals. *International Journal of Environmental Research and Public Health, 20*(1), Article 541. https://doi.org/10.3390/ijerph20010541

Kahn, W. A. (1990). Psychological conditions of personal engagement and disengagement at work. *Academy of Management Journal, 33*(4), 692–724.

Kanold, T. D., & Boogren, T. H. (2022). *Educator wellness: A guide for sustaining physical, mental, emotional, and social well-being.* Solution Tree Press.

Kashdan, T. B., Goodman, F. R., McKnight, P. E., Brown, B., & Rum, R. (2024). Purpose in life: A resolution on the definition, conceptual model, and optimal measurement. *American Psychologist, 79*(6), 838–853. https://doi.org/10.1037/amp0001223

Kenny, M. E., Medvide, M. B., & Gordon, P. (2024). Cultivating purpose and internalized motivation through workplace learning. *Gifted Education International, 40*(3), 295–311.

Khng, K. H. (2023). Deep breathing and mindfulness: Simple techniques to promote students' self-regulation and well-being from the inside out. In R. B. King, I. S. Caleon, & A. B. I. Bernardo (Eds.), *Positive psychology and positive education in Asia: Understanding and fostering well-being in schools* (pp. 311–325). Springer. https://doi.org/10.1007/978-981-999-5571-8_17

Koivunen, T., Pyöriä, P., & Saari, T. (2023). Job pride and work orientation among blue-collar workers in the Finnish vehicle industry. *International Journal of Sociology and Social Policy, 43*(13–14), 229–244.

Kosfeld, M., Neckermann, S., & Yang, X. (2017). The effects of financial and recognition incentives across work contexts: The role of meaning. *Economic Inquiry, 55*(1), 237–247.

Kraft, M. A., Blazar, D., & Hogan, D. (2018). The effect of teacher coaching on instruction and achievement: A meta-analysis of the causal evidence. *Review of Educational Research, 88*(4), 547–588.

Kraft, M. A., & Lyon, M. A. (2024). *The rise and fall of the teaching profession: Prestige, interest, preparation, and satisfaction over the last half century* (EdWorkingPaper No. 22-679). Annenberg Institute at Brown University. https://doi.org/10.26300/7b1a-vk92

Kraft, M. A., Marinell, W. H., & Yee, D. S.-W. (2016). School organizational contexts, teacher turnover, and student achievement: Evidence from panel data. *American Educational Research Journal, 53*(5), 1411–1449. https://doi.org/10.3102/0002831216667478

Kumari, P., & Niyogi, A. (2025). Crisis leadership and emotional climate: Lessons from post-pandemic educational settings. *Emotional Well-being and Mental Health in Higher Education*, 184.

Laslocky, M. (2021, April 30). *The mistake-friendly classroom.* Accessed at www.edutopia.org/article/mistake-friendly-classroom on December 10, 2025.

Leadership HQ. (2025). *Leadership. Neuroscience. Greatness* [Blog post]. Accessed at https://leadershiphq.com.au/leadership-neuroscience-greatness on December 10, 2025.

Li, X., Kuo, Y.-L., & Huggins, T. J. (2024). Perceived feedback and school belonging: The mediating role of subjective well-being. *Frontiers in Psychology, 15*, Article 1450788. Accessed at www.ncbi.nlm.nih.gov/pmc/articles/PMC11499173 on December 10, 2025.

Li, Y., & Singh, C. (2023). Impact of perceived recognition by physics instructors on women's self-efficacy and interest. *Physical Review Physics Education Research, 19*(2), Article 020125.

Logis, H. A., Ren, R., Hudgens, T. M., & Barnett, J. H. (2025). *NIET research summary: Examining the evidence and impact of NIET's initiatives—2024–25.* National Institute for Excellence in Teaching. Accessed at www.niet.org/assets/ResearchAndPolicyResources/2024-25-NIET-Research-Summary.pdf on December 10, 2025.

Lombard, E. (2022). Do you want this double or single spaced? Transactional versus transformational questions. *Journal of Education and Learning, 11*(5), 124–130. https://doi.org/10.5539/jel.v11n5p124

Mala, A. R., Abdullah, A. H., & Nento, S. (2022). The influence of supportive leadership behavior and organizational support on the job satisfaction of followers. *Al-Tanzim, 6*(4), 1247–1261. Accessed at https://ejournal.unuja.ac.id/index.php/al-tanzim/article/download/3528/pdf on December 10, 2025.

Malchelosse, K., Houlfort, N., Lavoie, C.-É., & Masson, R. (2024). The role of resilience and psychological needs satisfaction in the relationship between passion for work and work-life enrichment. *Current Psychology, 43*(7), 6640–6656. https://doi.org/10.1007/s12144-023-04846-0

Martela, F., Gómez, M., Unanue, W., Araya, S., Bravo, D., & Espejo, A. (2021). What makes work meaningful? Longitudinal evidence for the importance of autonomy and beneficence for meaningful work. *Journal of Vocational Behavior, 131*, Article 103631.

Martinsone, B., Di Sano, S., D'Elia, P., & La Salle-Finley, T. (2023). A conceptual framework for sustainable promotion of a positive school climate: Context, challenges, and solutions. *Journal of Teacher Education for Sustainability, 25*(1), 64–85.

Marzano, R. J., Warrick, P. B., & Acosta, M. I. (2024). *5 big ideas for leading a high reliability school.* Marzano Resources.

Maslach, C., & Leiter, M. P. (2016). Understanding the burnout experience: Recent research and its implications for psychiatry. *World Psychiatry, 15*(2), 103–111.

Matthews, R. A., Wayne, J. H., Smith, C., Casper, W. J., Wang, Y.-R., & Streit, J. (2022). Resign or carry-on? District and principal leadership as drivers of change in teacher turnover intentions during the COVID-19 crisis: A latent growth model examination. *Journal of Occupational and Organizational Psychology, 95*(3), 687–717.

McAdoo, J. (2025). The impact of vulnerable leadership on employee empowerment. *Open Journal of Business and Management, 13*(1), 1–23. https://doi.org/10.4236/ojbm.2025.131001

McKinsey & Company. (2023, July 17). *What is psychological safety?* Accessed at www.mckinsey.com/featured-insights/mckinsey-explainers/what-is-psychological-safety on December 10, 2025.

MENTOR. (2021). *Mentoring and education outcomes* (Research brief). Author. Accessed at www.mentoring.org/wp-content/uploads/2021/10/Mentoring-and-Educational-Outcomes.pdf on December 10, 2025.

Minahan, J., & Rappaport, N. (2012). *The behavior code: A practical guide to understanding and teaching the most challenging students.* Harvard Education Press.

Mohan, P., Pagidi, R. K., Ayyagiri, A., Goel, P., Jain, A., & Singh, S. P. (2024). Employee advocacy through automated HR solutions. *International Journal of Current Science, 14*(2), 24–41.

Mokracek, P., & Mohammed, L. A. (2022). Examining importance of respect in the classroom. *Journal of Emerging Technologies and Innovative Research, 9*(12), 545–552.

Mor, K., Gündemir, S., & van der Toorn, J. (2025). Celebrating the "invisible": The role of organizational diversity approaches on attracting and retaining LGBTQ+ talent. *Journal of Business and Psychology, 40*(3), 593–617. https://doi.org/10.1007/s10869-024-09975-2

Moreno, A. (2023). *Purpose-driven learning: Unlocking and empowering our students' innate passion for learning*. Routledge.

Morrill, C., & Musheno, M. (2018, March 27). *Culture of trust is key for school safety*. The Conversation. Accessed at https://theconversation.com/culture-of-trust-is-key-for-school-safety-92731 on December 11, 2025.

Müller, P. M., Behr, J., Yada, T., Eells, R., Leidig, T., & Hennemann, T. (2024). Collective teacher efficacy in context of students' externalizing behavior problems: A systematic review. *International Journal of Special Education, 39*(2), 126–147.

Mutonyi, B. R., Slåtten, T., Lien, G., & González-Piñero, M. (2022). The impact of organizational culture and leadership climate on organizational attractiveness and innovative behavior: A study of Norwegian hospital employees. *BMC Health Services Research, 22*(1), Article 637. https://doi.org/10.1186/s12913-022-08042-x

National Alliance for Public Charter Schools. (2023). *Elevating our voices: A guidebook for school-level teacher advocacy*. Author. Accessed at https://publiccharters.org/wp-content/uploads/2023/01/teacher-voice-toolkit_v2_0.pdf on December 11, 2025.

National Center for Education Statistics. (2023). *School Pulse Panel: Mental health services in public schools*. U.S. Department of Education, Institute of Education Sciences. Accessed at https://nces.ed.gov/surveys/spp on April 7, 2026.

National Education Association. (2020). *Great teaching and learning: Creating the culture to support professional excellence*. Author. Accessed at www.nea.org/sites/default/files/2020-06/Great%20Teaching%20and%20Learning%20Report.pdf on December 10, 2025.

Ocobock, C., Niclou, A., Loewen, T., Arslanian, K., Gibson, R., & Valeggia, C. (2022). Demystifying mentorship: Tips for successfully navigating the mentor–mentee journey. *American Journal of Human Biology, 34*(S1), Article e23690.

OpenAI. (2025a, May 4). *School climate research and discovery* [Generative AI chat]. ChatGPT. https://chatgpt.com/g/g-p-67e1a38042e48191a06fcab2ac23ccf5/c/6817e039-68c4-8009-bf5a-b7b9d492ed23.

OpenAI. (2025b, November 20). *AI prompts for strategies* [Generative AI chat]. ChatGPT. https://chatgpt.com/g/g-p-67e1a38042e48191a06fcab2ac23ccf5-reimagining-school-climate/c/691fb224-fb9c-8328-8198-566ac8b8a10e.

Osher, D., & Berg, J. (2018). *School climate and social and emotional learning: The integration of two approaches* [Issue brief]. Pennsylvania State University. Accessed at www.air.org/sites/default/files/2021-06/School-Climate-and-Social-and-Emotional-Learning-Integrative-Approach-January-2018.pdf on December 11, 2025.

Overstreet, S., & Chafouleas, S. M. (2016). Trauma-informed schools: Introduction to the special issue. *School Mental Health, 8*(1), 1–6. https://doi.org/10.1007/s12310-016-9184-1

Patzak, A., & Zhang, X. (2025). Blending teacher autonomy support and provision of structure in the classroom for optimal motivation: A systematic review and metaanalysis. *Educational Psychology Review, 37*(1), Article 17. https://doi.org/10.1007/s10648-025-09994-2

Peetz Stephens, C., & Baker, L. (2024, April 26). What schools can do to make sure support staff feel appreciated. *Education Week*. Accessed at www.edweek.org/leadership/what-schools-can-do-to-make-sure-support-staff-feel-appreciated/2024/04 on December 11, 2025.

Peist, E., McMahon, S. D., Davis-Wright, J. O., & Keys, C. B. (2024). Understanding teacher-directed violence and related turnover through a school climate framework. *Psychology in the Schools*, *61*(1), 220–236. https://doi.org/10.1002/pits.23044

Phan, M. L., Renshaw, T. L., Domenech Rodríguez, M. M., McClain, M. B., Moo, E. L., Humphries, A., & Parker, B. (2025). Evaluating the effects of a teacher-implemented mindfulness-based intervention on teacher stress and student prosocial behavior. *Contemporary School Psychology*, *29*(2), 393–409. https://doi.org/10.1007/s40688-025-00540-z

Pierantoni, R. (2017, February 15). *How classroom predictability and student trust enhance student learning* [Blog post]. Accessed at https://njalternateroute.rutgers.edu/blog/how-classroom-predictability-student-trust-enhance-student-learning on December 10, 2025.

Pincus, J. D. (2023). Well-being as need fulfillment: Implications for theory, methods, and practice. *Integrative Psychological and Behavioral Sciences*, *58*(4), 1541–1579.

Pindek, S., Zhou, Z. E., Kessler, S. R., Krajcevska, A., & Spector, P. E. (2021). Workdays are not created equal: Job satisfaction and job stressors across the workweek. *Human Relations*, *74*(9), 1447–1472.

Putra, S., Setiadi, N. J., Gautama, I., Bandur, A., & Sundjaja, A. M. (2025). The relationship between leadership, psychological safety, and innovation: A bibliometric review analysis. *International Journal of Innovative Research and Scientific Studies*, *8*(3), 2240–2254.

Quaglia, R. J., & Corso, M. J. (2014). *Student voice: The instrument of change*. Corwin Press.

Rapa, L. J., Katsiyannis, A., Scott, S. N., & Durham, O. (2024). School shootings in the United States: 1997–2022. *Pediatrics*, *153*(4), e2023064311.

Rasheed, K., Rehan, Q., Khan, T., Tabassum, R., Irfan, M., Khan, K., et al. (2024). Relationship between ethical leadership practices, positive school climate, and trust in leaders in public schools of Lahore. *Journal of Tianjin University of Science and Technology*, *57*(10), 27–48.

Ravishankar, S., Spencer-Drakes, T. C. J., Fernandes, I. H., Hayes, M. I., Coopwood, S., Spencer, I., et al. (2024). Empowering STEM students: A university-wide mentorship program fostering retention and belonging. *Journal of Cellular Physiology*, *239*(7), Article e31348.

Ray, T. K., & Pana-Cryan, R. (2021). Work flexibility and work-related well-being. *International Journal of Environmental Research and Public Health*, *18*(6), Article 3254.

Reeve, J., & Cheon, S. H. (2021). Autonomy-supportive teaching: Its malleability, benefits, and potential to improve educational practice. *Educational Psychologist*, *56*(1), 54–77.

Reisinger, J. (2024, September 13). *Educator well-being: The foundation of school well-being* [Blog post]. Accessed at www.erblearn.org/blog/teacher-self-care-educator-well-being on December 11, 2025.

Ruzek, J. I. (2025). Social group interventions to increase resilience and stress resistance in an era of increasing adversity. *Journal of Aggression, Maltreatment and Trauma*, *34*(7), 1049–1067.

Ryan, R. M., & Deci, E. L. (2017). *Self-determination theory: Basic psychological needs in motivation, development, and wellness.* Guilford Press.

Ryan, R. M., & Deci, E. L. (2020). Intrinsic and extrinsic motivation from a self-determination theory perspective: Definitions, theory, practices, and future directions. *Contemporary Educational Psychology, 61*, 101860.

Savill-Smith, C., & Scanlan, D. (2022). *Teacher Wellbeing Index 2022.* Education Support. Accessed at www.educationsupport.org.uk/media/zoga2r13/teacher-wellbeing-index-2022.pdf on December 9, 2025.

Schneider, B., Ehrhart, M. G., & Macey, W. H. (2011). Perspectives on organizational climate and culture. In S. Zedeck (Ed.), *APA handbook of industrial and organizational psychology, volume 1. Building and developing the organization* (pp. 373–414). American Psychological Association. https://doi.org/10.1037/12169-012

Schulze-Hagenest, T., Carstensen, B., Weber, K., Jansen, T., Meyer, J., Köller, O., & Klusmann, U. (2023). Teachers' emotional exhaustion and job satisfaction: How much does the school context matter? *Teaching and Teacher Education, 136*, Article 104360. https://doi.org/10.1016/j.tate.2023.104360

Seligman, M. (2018). PERMA and the building blocks of well-being. *The Journal of Positive Psychology, 13*(4), 333–335.

Shahid, S., & Din, M. (2021). Fostering psychological safety in teachers: The role of school leadership, team effectiveness and organizational culture. *International Journal of Educational Leadership in Management, 9*(2), 122–149.

Shanafelt, T., Trockel, M., Wang, H., Mayer, T., & Athey, L. (2022). Assessing professional fulfillment and burnout among CEOs and other healthcare administrative leaders in the United States. *Journal of Healthcare Management, 67*(5), 317–338. https://doi.org/10.1097/JHM-D-22-00012

Sharma, D., Gupta, S., & Verma, D. (2025). Emotional intelligence in the age of digital intelligence. In P. K. Dutta, S. Gupta, S. Kashyap, A. Gehlot, R. Karmakar, & P. Bhattacharya (Eds.), *Emotional intelligence in the digital era* (pp. 1–15). CRC Press.

Sharma, G., Yukhymenko-Lescroart, M., & Sanchez, T. (2023). Examining the role of life purpose in high school students' self-esteem through structural equation modelling. *Heliyon, 9*(9), Article e19614.

Skaalvik, E. M., & Skaalvik, S. (2017). Motivated for teaching? Associations with school goal structure, teacher self-efficacy, job satisfaction, and emotional exhaustion. *Teaching and Teacher Education, 67*, 152–160. https://doi.org/10.1016/j.tate.2017.06.006

Skaalvik, E. M., & Skaalvik, S. (2020). Teacher burnout: Relations between dimensions of burnout, perceived school context, job satisfaction and motivation for teaching. A longitudinal study. *Teachers and Teaching, 26*(7–8), 602–616.

Slil, E., Iyiola, K., Alzubi, A., & Aljuhmani, H. Y. (2025). Impact of safety leadership and employee morale on safety performance: The moderating role of harmonious safety passion. *Buildings, 15*(2), Article 186. https://doi.org/10.3390/buildings15020186

Smith, E. N., Rozek, C. S., Manke, K. J., Dweck, C. S., & Walton, G. M. (2021). Teacher versus researcher-provided affirmation effects on students' task engagement and positive perceptions of teachers. *Journal of Social Issues, 77*(3), 751–768. https://doi.org/10.1111/josi.12417

Sokoloff, N. (2025, May 13). CT lawmakers pass sweeping education bill, with changes to cellphone use, crisis drills and more. *CT Insider*. Accessed at www.ctinsider.com/news/education/article/ct-education-legislation-2025-drills-cellphone-law-20324780.php on December 11, 2025.

Steiner, E. D., Woo, A., Suryavanshi, A., & Redding, C. (2023). *Working conditions related to positive teacher well-being vary across states: Findings from the 2022 Learn Together Survey* (Report No. RR-A827-15). RAND. Accessed at www.rand.org/pubs/research_reports/RRA827-15.html on December 11, 2025.

Stone, D., & Heen, S. (2014). *Thanks for the feedback: The science and art of receiving feedback well (even when it is off base, unfair, poorly delivered, and frankly, you're not in the mood)*. Viking.

Strobel Education. (2023, October 23). *The impact of school climate on well-being* [Blog post]. Accessed at https://strobeleducation.com/blog/the-impact-of-school-climate-on-well-being on December 11, 2025.

Stutey, D. M., Solis, A. E., Severn, K., Notestine, L., Enkler, K. L., Wehrman, J., & Cammell, M. (2022). Perceptions of at-promise youth in a therapeutic youth mentoring program. *The Professional Counselor, 12*(1), 17–35. https://doi.org/10.15241/dms.12.1.17

Sullins, J., Turner, J., Kim, J., & Barber, S. (2024). Investigating the impacts of shame-proneness on students' state shame, self-regulation, and learning. *Education Sciences, 14*(2), Article 138. https://doi.org/10.3390/educsci14020138

Täschner, J., Dicke, T., Reinhold, S., & Holzberger, D. (2025). "Yes, I can!" A systematic review and meta-analysis of intervention studies promoting teacher self-efficacy. *Review of Educational Research, 95*(1), 3–52.

Terrell, R. D., Terrell, E. K., Lindsey, R. B., & Lindsey, D. B. (2018). *Culturally proficient leadership: The personal journey begins within*. Corwin Press.

Theoharis, G. (2024). *The school leaders our children deserve: Seven keys to equity, social justice, and school reform*. Teachers College Press.

Tracy, J. L., Mercadante, J. A., & Hohm, I. (2023). Pride: The emotional foundation of social rank attainment. *Annual Review of Psychology, 74*, 519–545. https://doi.org/10.1146/annurev-psych-032720-040321

U.S. Department of Education. (2021). *Supporting child and student social, emotional, behavioral, and mental health needs*. Author. Accessed at www.ed.gov/sites/ed/files/documents/students/supporting-child-student-social-emotional-behavioral-mental-health.pdf on December 11, 2025.

U.S. Department of Education. (2025). *K-12 cybersecurity: Learn how ED supports K–12 cybersecurity resilience*. Accessed at www.ed.gov/teaching-and-administration/safe-learning-environments/school-safety-and-security/k-12-cybersecurity on December 11, 2025.

Van der Kolk, B. A. (2014). *The body keeps the score: Brain, mind, and body in the healing of trauma*. Viking.

Veletić, J., Price, H. E., & Olsen, R. V. (2023). Teachers' and principals' perceptions of school climate: The role of principals' leadership style in organizational quality. *Educational Assessment, Evaluation and Accountability, 35*(4), 525–555.

Vijai, C. (2025). The relationship between emotional intelligence, transformational leadership, and organizational culture. In P. K. Dutta, S. Gupta, S. Kashyap, A. Gehlot, R. Karmakar, & P. Bhattacharya (Eds.), *Emotional intelligence in the digital era* (pp. 212–237). CRC Press.

Wang, M. T., Degol, J. L., & Henry, D. A. (2019). An integrative development-in-sociocultural-context model for children's engagement in learning. *American Psychologist, 74*(9), 1086.

Wang, X., Yang, L., Chen, K., & Zheng, Y. (2023). Understanding teacher emotional exhaustion: Exploring the role of teaching motivation, perceived autonomy, and teacher–student relationships. *Frontiers in Psychology, 14*, Article 1342598.

Weller Swanson, K., & Caskey, M. M. (2024). Community of practice mentoring to retain middle school teachers. *Current Issues in Middle Level Education, 28*(1), Article 4.

Weziak-Bialowolska, D., Lee, M. T., Bialowolski, P., McNeely, E., Chen, Y., Cowden, R. G., et al. (2023). Associations between the importance of well-being domains and the subsequent experience of well-being. *Sustainability, 15*(1), Article 594. https://doi.org/10.3390/su15010594

Wowor, J. V., & Dewi, Y. E. P. (2022). The influence of psychological safety towards employee engagement using organizational support as intervening variable. *Andalas Management Review, 6*(2), 32–42. https://doi.org/10.25077/amar.6.2.48-58.2022

Xanthopoulou, P. I., Patitsa, C. D., Sotiropoulou, K., Chalaris, M., & Kalogiannidis, S. (2025). Factors of work-related stress: The impact of work stress on the performance and well-being of public sector employees. In M. Pazarskis, A. Kostyuk, V. Santolamazza, & P. Capuano (Eds.), *Corporate governance: Scholarly research and practice* (pp. 112–116). Virtus Interpress. https://doi.org/10.22495/cgsrapp22

Xu, G., Haratyan, F., & Tian, H. (2026). A 2025 systematic review of teacher emotion regulation and well-being: Implications for student engagement, learning outcomes, and professional development in EFL contexts. *Frontiers in Psychology, 16*, 1715266.

Yeager, D. S., Dahl, R. E., & Dweck, C. S. (2017). Why interventions to influence adolescent behavior often fail but could succeed. *Perspectives on Psychological Science, 13*(1), 101–122.

Zhang, S., & Luo, Y. (2023). Review on the conceptual framework of teacher resilience. *Frontiers in Psychology, 14*, Article 1179984. https://doi.org/10.3389/fpsyg.2023.1179984

Index